Reforming Worship

Reforming Worship

English Reformed Principles and Practice

JULIAN TEMPLETON AND KEITH RIGLIN, EDITORS

WIPF & STOCK · Eugene, Oregon

REFORMING WORSHIP
English Reformed Principles and Practice

Wipf & Stock
An Imprint of Wipf and Stock Publishers
199 W. 8th Ave., Suite 3
Eugene, OR 97401
www.wipfandstock.com

ISBN 13: 978-1-61097-320-5

Manufactured in the U.S.A.

Biblical quotations are from the following translations:

New Revised Standard Version of the Bible, Anglicized edition, copyright © 1989, 1995
by the Division of Christian Education of the National Council of the Churches of
Christ in the USA. Used by permission. All rights reserved.

Revised English Bible, a revision of the New English Bible, 1970, copyright © Oxford
University Press and Cambridge University Press, 1989.

Revised Standard Version of the Bible, copyright © 1952, 2nd edition 1971, by the
Division of Christian Education of the National Council of the Churches of Christ in
the USA. Used by permission. All rights reserved.

Quotations of Psalms 42 and 51 from *Psalter Hymnal* (1987) used with permission of
"Faith Alive Christian Resources."

Quotation of Psalm 134 from *Psalter Hymnal* (1987) used with permission of Calvin
Seerveld.

Quotations from *Worship: from the United Reformed Church* (2003–4) used with
permission of the United Reformed Church, United Kingdom.

JT
to Laura Templeton
and Janice and the late Desmond Templeton

KR
to Jennifer Smith
and John Morgan-Wynne

Contents

Foreword

by Angela Tilby

How do twenty-first century Christians worship Almighty God? How do the abiding theological principles of Christian worship translate to our age? The questions raised by this collection of essays are relevant to all those seeking to be sensitive to both the traditions they have received from the past and the opportunities and difficulties that challenge Christians now.

Reading, or rather, re-discovering these rich and varied reflections—I was an Anglican participant at the conference that was the genesis of this book—I am struck by how universal the issues are. Like Ernest Marvin, whose plea for the church to "shape-up" sets a challenge which shapes much of what follows, I have gritted my teeth at lavishly-produced "praise and prayer" services which mimic mass-media events and seem principally designed to produce an intense emotional high for the participants. The theology behind such styles of worship is not easy to identify, but it does seem to be more about the worshippers' feelings— it is all about *me*—rather than about the God of Sinai and Calvary.

So it is appropriate that many of these reflections seek to re-ground Reformed worship in the history and story of the churches themselves. What emerges as a major concern is the tension between order and freedom in worship. Finding a fruitful pathway between total prescription and charismatic spontaneity has never been easy. The characteristic Reformed approach of ordered freedom is highlighted here. This is a much more fruitful way of describing what is going on in the worship of the churches of the Reformation, including that of the Church of England, than the potentially polemical contrast that has been made (and sometimes still is) between worship which is driven by liturgical texts and that which depends more on spontaneity. Ordered freedom could well apply to both. The point is that it is worship that rests in and grows out of a deep familiarity with the Scriptures. It is supported by a habit of life in which it is normal to "hear them, read, mark, learn, and inwardly digest them"[1] as God's life-giving Word.

One of the great problems for the churches of the Reformation nowadays is that contemporary congregations are much less familiar with Scripture than their forebears were. This has not been helped by the multiplicity of translations, which, through their sheer diversity and varying quality, have virtually killed off the scriptural memory and resonance on which our Christian formation has so long depended and which has played such an important part in our cultural history. Even in the 1960s it was possible for the BBC television revue *Beyond the Fringe* to parody the story of Jacob and Esau ("Esau was an hairy man . . .") because the poetry of the Genesis story in the Authorized Version (the "King James Bible"), even if it was not widely known, was recognized. Today the parody would have been incomprehensible. So how does Scripture live in the worship of today's church? How does it call us to a God who is kind, merciful and generous; but also holy, majestic and beyond all description? It is a cheap answer to reduce what we pray and proclaim about God to the bland, banal, and easily believable.

The second area, which is explored here in various ways, is that of inclusivity. This is a cardinal virtue for present-day society and an aspiration taken very seriously by the churches. For some, women in particular, the gendered language of orthodox faith is problematic. For others, the sacraments create difficulties. Who may preside at Holy Communion? Who may receive and who should not? Given the level of commitment implied by Holy Communion is it better to restrict it to rare occasions? Does Communion make evangelism more difficult?

The underlying issue here is discerning at what level worship relies on the keeping of boundaries and distinctions and when the inclusivity of the Lord's invitation should take priority over all human dogma and rule-making. Julian Templeton draws on evidence to suggest that the Trinity itself subverts the typical hierarchies of human power-mongering; but the challenge remains of how trinitarian faith is made real and vital in contemporary language and patterns of worship. Forms of

---

1 Collect for the 2nd Sunday in Advent, *Book of Common Prayer.*

prayer that set out to be inclusive are too often inclined to be vague, adopting an aspirational non-offensive tone that avoids the specificity and scriptural precision that would make them potentially transformative. The issue leads back to the center, to the nature of God. For those in the wider tradition of the Reformation, as for those whose leanings are more specifically Calvinistic, the challenge of worship is to learn to respond with praise, gratitude and self-sacrifice to the free and sovereign grace of God. It is good that this collection concludes with an invitation to sing the psalms as they were sung in Geneva, a stirring sermon and some patterns for prayer.

The revival of our worship depends on a rediscovery of the mystery at the heart of life, and that will only grow from a profound and disciplined attentiveness to the sources of faith in Scripture and in the on-going tradition of faith in the Christian community. This collection of writings is evidence of such attentiveness.

Oxford, 2011

Contributors

The Reverend Dr David Cornick is a minister of the United Reformed Church. He is the General Secretary of Churches Together in England, and a fellow of Robinson College, Cambridge. He has served as Principal of Westminster College, Cambridge, and as the General Secretary of the United Reformed Church. His publications include *Under God's Good Hand* (1998) and *Letting God be God* (2008).

Barbara Douglas is a musician, mother, and scholar whose interests have led her to investigate music for worship in general and Reformed psalmody in particular. Brought up in the Dutch Reformed tradition, she trained as a musician at the University of Iowa, and studied the aesthetics of music at the Institute for Christian Studies in Toronto. She contributed to the volume, *Pledges of Jubilee: Essays on the Arts and Culture* (1995).

The Reverend Fleur Houston is a minister of the United Reformed Church, and has served churches in Sheffield and Oxford. She holds degrees in French from Aberdeen and Oxford universities and in theology from Cambridge. For many years she has enjoyed a close association with members, councils, and thinkers of the Reformed Church of France.

Richard Howard was, for three years, a United Reformed Church minister serving in Chester, where he was the pastor of two congregations. In 2009 he became a Roman Catholic. He is now training to become a priest for the Roman Catholic Diocese of Shrewsbury in England. He is presently studying at the International Seminary of the Society of St John Mary Vianney in France.

The Reverend Ernest Marvin is a minister of the United Reformed Church, a former minister of St Columba's Church, Cambridge, and former Church of Scotland chaplain to the University of

Cambridge. He is the co-lyricist of the influential rock musical *A Man Dies* (1960) and author of *Shaping Up—Re-forming Reformed Worship* (2005). He has been an annual visitor to the USA over the last forty years where he has preached and lectured in churches, seminaries, and universities from Boston to San Francisco.

The Reverend Dr Keith Riglin has served in Baptist and United Reformed charges in Bath, Amersham, and Fulbourn, as minister and university chaplain at St Columba's Church, Cambridge, and as a lecturer at the United Theological College of the West Indies, Jamaica. He is a graduate of London, Oxford, and Birmingham universities, and a senior member of Wolfson College, Cambridge. He contributed to the volume, *Mary for Earth and Heaven: Essays on Mary and Ecumenism* (2002). He is now an Anglican priest serving in the Diocese of London.

The Reverend Julian Templeton is a minister of the United Reformed Church, serving congregations in Highgate and New Barnet, London. He is a graduate in music and divinity from the University of Otago and was ordained by the Presbyterian Church of Aotearoa New Zealand. Upon emigrating to the United Kingdom he entered the United Reformed Church, undertook post-graduate research at King's College London, and was for seven years Assistant Director of Ministerial Training at Mansfield College, Oxford.

The Reverend Dr Colin Thompson is a minister of the United Reformed Church. He is a fellow of St Catherine's College, Oxford, and Faculty Lecturer in Spanish, University of Oxford. His publications include *St John of the Cross: Songs in the Night* (2002) and *La lucha de las lenguas: Fray Luis de León y el Siglo de Oro en España* (1995).

The Reverend Professor David Thompson is Emeritus Professor of Modern Church History in the University of Cambridge, and a minister of the United Reformed Church. He was Convenor of the Editorial Committee for the United Reformed Church hymn-book, *Rejoice and Sing* (1991) and was Moderator of the General Assembly of the United Reformed Church, 1996–97. His most recent publications include *Cambridge Theology in the Nineteenth Century* (2008) and an essay in *Dissenting Praise* (2011) entitled "Finding Successors to 'the Poet of the Sanctuary': Josiah Conder in Context".

The Reverend Canon Angela Tilby is Diocesan Canon of Christ Church, Oxford, and Continuing Ministerial Development Advisor for the Diocese of Oxford. A regular contributor to BBC Radio 4's "Thought for the Day," she was formerly Vicar of St Bene't's Church, Cambridge, and Vice-Principal of Westcott House, Cambridge. Her publications include: *The Seven Deadly Sins* (2009) and *Everyday Prayer: Praying with the Church* (2006).

Abbreviations

ARIC	Anglican-Reformed International Commission
CRC	Christian Reformed Church (USA)
CTBI	Churches Together in Britain and Ireland
CUP	Cambridge University Press
NRSV	New Revised Standard Version
OUP	Oxford University Press
REB	Revised English Bible
RSV	Revised Standard Version
URC	United Reformed Church (UK)
WCC	World Council of Churches

1

Ordered Freedom: English Reformed Worship

BY JULIAN TEMPLETON AND KEITH RIGLIN

THE CONTRIBUTIONS TO THIS volume originate from a conference that took place at Westminster College, Cambridge, England, in September 2007. The title of the conference was *Reforming Worship: Reformed Principles and Practice.* Fifty participants came, mostly from England, and of these most were ministers of the United Reformed Church.[1] Over four days they listened, debated, ate, and worshipped in a college near the River Cam in the environs of the university and city of Cambridge. What drew them together was a common interest in Reformed worship. However, about what constitutes, or should constitute, Reformed worship today, much was contested. This is hardly surprising, coming from a tradition that David Cornick argues, ". . . was polyphonous, maybe even cacophonous, from its birth."[2] Due to England's peculiar religious and political history, these many and competing voices have, if anything, been amplified. Whilst acknowledging that an agreement about what constitutes Reformed worship in England is more of an aspiration than a reality; as editors, we have nonetheless discerned in the contributions to this collection some common threads that we shall consider under the heading of *Ordered Freedom.*

The content and form of worship has been at the forefront of reforms of the Western church for at least the past 500 years, from the Protestant Reformation, the "Counter-Reformation" in the Church of

---

1. Formed in 1972 by the union of the Congregational Church in England and Wales with the Presbyterian Church of England. It was joined in 1981 by the Churches of Christ, and in 2000 by the Congregational Union of Scotland.

2. Page 22.

Rome, the reforms of the Second Vatican Council, to the ecumenical liturgical cross-fertilization evident in the twentieth century. The fact that worship has been the vanguard of reform is not surprising, since the worship of God is the central and defining activity of the church. Worship is the act in which the church encounters and glorifies the triune God who creates, redeems, and reconciles the world. This is why worship is the hub from which all other aspects of the church's life radiate.

The majority of the contributors to this collection of essays identify with the Reformed stream of the church that commonly found its expression in the English-speaking world under the titles Congregational and Presbyterian.[3] Huldrych Zwingli in Zurich, Martin Bucer in Strasbourg, John Calvin in Geneva, Thomas Cranmer and other Anglican divines in England,[4] and John Knox in Scotland were all much-influenced by the German reformer Martin Luther. They led and inspired thoroughgoing reforms of the church, centered on worship. The Reformed approach is perhaps best encapsulated in the phrase, *Ecclesia reformata, semper reformanda*, "The church reformed, always to be reformed" according to the Word of God.[5] *Semper reformanda* gives rise to the title of this collection of essays: *Reforming Worship*. We believe that one of the contributions of Reformed Christians to the church catholic is a tradition of worship reformed in ever-new obedience to the Word of God and leading of the Holy Spirit. This reforming of worship is the demanding task of discerning how best to be faithful to the Word of God in the ever-changing confluence of culture and time.[6] By the "Word of God" the Reformed have meant, in the first instance, the Scriptures. Thus the reading and preaching of the Scriptures is central to Reformed worship.

3. At least since 1662 in England these two traditions, together with the Baptists— who, apart from their distinctive baptismal practice have remained essentially Congregationalist—have been identified (and often self-identified) as Nonconformists or, with the Methodists, collectively as the "Free Churches."

4. The "Reformed" character of the Church of England may be perceived in both its *Articles of Religion* (1562) and its *Book of Common Prayer* (1662).

5. "The church, in obedience to Jesus Christ, is open to the reform of its standards of doctrine as well as of governance. The church affirms *ecclesia reformata, semper reformanda*, that is, 'the church reformed, always reforming,' according to the Word of God and the call of the Spirit." Presbyterian Church (USA), *Book of Order*, paragraph G-2.0300.

6. Expressed in the United Reformed Church statement, "The highest authority for what we believe and do is God's Word in the Bible alive for his people today through the help of the Spirit." *The Basis of Union*, The Manual, 13.

For many years Reformed worshippers sang only the Scriptures (almost exclusively, the Psalms: see essay by Barbara Douglas).[7] However, it was the English Congregationalist minister, Isaac Watts, who in his paraphrases of the Psalms for singing in worship, felt free to ". . . teach my author to speak like a Christian." Watts is a pivotal figure in the enlargement of the English-speaking churches' sung repertoire to include non-Psalm-based hymns.

The generalization that the Scriptures shape the content of Reformed worship to a substantial extent still holds true today. That said, none of the early Reformed leaders subscribed to the view, held by some, that being faithful to the Scriptures necessarily involved the abolition of all the traditions of the church catholic. Rather, they believed the church needed to reform and purify those accretions and abuses that obscured the gospel.[8] The reform of worship according to the Scriptures was where many started. Martin Bucer and John Calvin advocated (from Acts 2:42) that all worship should consist of (i) reading and teaching the scriptures, (ii) fellowship and almsgiving, (iii) the "breaking of bread" or baptism, (iv) prayer and praise. This brings us to the first mark of Reformed worship: *orderliness*. Reformed worshippers have taken the apostle Paul's exhortation to the church at Corinth that their worship should proceed ". . . decently and in order"[9] as a maxim. Reformed worship is ordered worship. This is not to suggest that its sequence is always the same—though often it is—it is to say that in Reformed worship certain essential elements will always be present. The Scriptures will be read and preached; praise and prayer will be offered; money will be collected for particular needs; the common life of the fellowship will be renewed; and the Lord's Supper, even when not celebrated, sounds its dominant note of thanksgiving.

Within this order there is much scope for the second mark of Reformed worship: *freedom*. Reformed worshippers have taken as a maxim another of the apostle's reflections, ". . . where the Spirit of the

---

7. See pages 129–149.

8. Later generations of the Reformed were not so subtle, so that, whereas in Lutheran churches a tradition developed of only removing from the received tradition of the medieval church that specifically forbidden by Scripture—thus much of the color and ritual of the liturgy remained—in Reformed churches the tradition soon developed of only permitting that which the Scriptures specifically allowed.

9. 1 Cor 14:40 REB.

Lord is, there is freedom."[10] Reformed worshippers have not strictly adhered to a standard written liturgy or prayer book.[11] This is because the Reformed believe that worshippers and presiders at worship should be free to respond to the leading of the Holy Spirit. In saying this, however, we would not wish to give the impression that spontaneity predominates. Rather, it means that Reformed leaders of worship are free to prepare and use newly-composed prayers and liturgies for each act of worship, often shaped by the theme of the sermon, which is itself shaped by the scriptural message.

Reformed worship, then, is characterized by an *ordered freedom*. Whilst order and freedom in worship are sometimes thought to be opposed, there is nonetheless a necessary symbiosis between them. Order without freedom risks becoming boring and stifling. Freedom without order risks becoming confusing and chaotic. Ordered worship provides the framework, and therefore the freedom, within which worshippers may both encounter and respond to the living God. Reformed worship in the English-speaking world has mostly steered a middle course between the standard liturgies of the liturgical churches and the spontaneous freedom of the independent churches. The ordered freedom of Reformed worship is, however, not without its tensions. These tensions are exemplified by the Westminster Assembly's 1645 *Directory for the Public Worship of God*. The *Directory* attempted to regulate worship in England, Scotland, and Ireland by combining ". . . order and liberty, form and the spirit, unity and variety, hitherto deemed incompatible and certainly estranged."[12] It is essentially a compromise between the Presbyterian concern for order and the Independent demand for freedom. The tension involved in maintaining this compromise can be evidenced in this: what began as a revision of the *Book of Common Prayer* ended as a directory that ". . . consists of nothing but rubrics."[13]

10. 2 Cor 3:17 NRSV.

11. Even some of the notable exceptions, such as Orchard's experiments at the King's Weigh House, London—discussed in David Cornick's essay—were "free" in that their adoption was the free choice of the congregation's "church meeting."

12. Davies, *Worship and Theology in England. From Cranmer to Baxter and Fox*, 409.

13. See Page 32. Much "catholic" form is retained in the first *Book of Common Order* of the Church of Scotland (also known as *Knox's Liturgy*) of 1556 and all subsequent editions—the latest being that of 1994. From this perspective, the Directory tradition, dominant for so long in the English-speaking Reformed tradition, may be regarded as

Many of the essays in this collection bear witness to the on-going tension between freedom and order. Ernest Marvin argues that Scripture provides the Reformed with principles of order that temper the exercise of freedom in worship, with the warning: "When the church is careless of form and order, unnecessary distractions enter in and the descent into kitsch is close at hand."[14] In Julian Templeton's analysis of a recent liturgical resource produced by the United Reformed Church, he discerns a tension between the order of orthodox Trinitarian doctrine, on the one hand; and the freedom to make references to God gender-inclusive, on the other. Keith Riglin's essay[15] exposes the disorder—justified in the name of freedom—caused by inadvertent or deliberate laxity about who is authorized to preside at the Eucharist. Fleur Houston explores the tension between Barth's hermeneutic of the revelatory order demanded by the Word of God and Ricoeur's hermeneutic of the freedom of biblically-inspired imagination.[16] David Thompson discusses the tension between the freely-extended invitation to all the baptized to share in Holy Communion and the desire to guard against disorder in the fellowship by requiring personal examination from those who come to the Lord's table.[17] Richard Howard continues along similar lines when he analyses the tension between the Reformed (and Protestant) understanding of the once-for-all, sufficient sacrifice of Christ and the church's ongoing sacrifice offered in union with Christ's eternal offering of himself to God the Father.[18] Colin Thompson, in a sermon, describes the tension we have been exploring as *creative space*:

> . . . between language which imagines God and language which is wholly inadequate to do more than stammer; between a sense of our own limitations and unworthiness and the call of God which takes us as we are; between the earthbound and the heavenly; between freedom and order; between the culture of our age and the principles of theology; between our particular traditions and the one holy catholic and apostolic Church through the ages and in the new Jerusalem. If we can accept such tensions as gifts to

---

a departure, albeit one lasting for generations.

14. Page 16.

15. See pages 62–83.

16. See pages 84–94.

17. See pages 95–112.

18. See pages 113–28.

be shared rather than possessions to be defended, and if we can
explore the terrain they offer, in humility and with a listening ear,
doors will open, paths will be smoothed, and our worship will
lead us to grow, however imperceptibly, towards the fullness of
the stature of Christ . . . [19]

A common theme running through all the essays is the desire to
address issues not from a narrow denominational perspective but from
that of the great church, catholic and Reformed. Theology that is con-
textual demands illustrations from and examinations of the particular
expressions of the Reformed tradition in which the authors have all
ministered, but it also demands reflections that, we trust, are insightful
for all.

All our contributors, however, whilst noting tensions between a
freedom that can become unbridled license and an order that can become uncritical conformity, do not subscribe to a view that there is any
tension between the church as catholic and the church as Reformed.
Rather, our bold contention is that *ordered freedom* is the scriptural mark
of the church's worship, and the character of *all* good liturgy. We contend
that this is true of all communions, be they Anglican, Protestant, Roman
Catholic, or Orthodox.

Not for nothing, therefore, does this collection begin with a foreword from the Anglican preacher, liturgist, and writer, Angela Tilby,
and conclude with examples of worship—in sung psalms, a sermon, and
liturgies—from the Reformed tradition. Our conviction remains that, to
paraphrase the *Shorter Catechism*, our purpose in life as human beings
is to worship God and fully to delight in God forever.[20]

---

19. Page 152.

20. "Man's chief end is to glorify God, and to enjoy him for ever." *The Shorter
Catechism* of the Westminster Assembly, 1647.

2

Shaping Up: Re-forming Reformed Worship[1]

BY ERNEST MARVIN

DAVID ONLY CAME OCCASIONALLY to church. He was seventeen and had a different agenda from that of his parents, albeit one shared with the majority of his peers. It was obvious that when he did come it was only out of respect and affection for the former, which was no bad thing. "David," I ventured to say one Sunday morning during coffee hour, "I notice you never sing the hymns; why not?" He replied, "I only sing when I'm happy and I'm never happy in church." There was no answer to that, or at least none that could have progressed very far in the midst of the post-cultus chatter around the fair-trade stall.

Worship is a response, a response to a persistent claim upon our lives, but if no claim is felt then no positive response is possible. Of course the experience of a strong claim upon one's life is not the sole preserve of the religiously inclined. It may have its source in another human being—"I worship the ground she walks on"—or it may originate from witnessing a beautiful sunset or hearing a stunning piece of music—"It took me out of myself"—and so on. But the particular activity in which Christians, Jews, Muslims, Hindus, and many others engage and speak of as worship certainly differs in kind, if not always in degree, from this at the human level. Most religions assert that their worship is a response to a reality that is beyond. It was this experience that David honestly confessed was not his and therefore he could not, with equal honesty, respond to it with praise. It was interesting nonetheless that he associated

1. This chapter is a development of the opening address given at the *Reforming Worship* conference of 2007. The ideas are further developed in Marvin, *Shaping Up*.

the state of being happy as a prerequisite for the act of worship. This is a mistake that is also commonly made by some Christians, hence those fixed smiles that can make some of us squirm.

Why do Christians worship God, albeit often in different ways? We do so because we believe our God created us for that purpose. As the answer to the first question of the Westminster *Shorter Catechism* puts it, "Man's [sic] chief and highest end is to glorify God, and fully to enjoy him forever."[2] We believe that God created us in his image, and one that would reflect his glory. We also believe that God commanded our worship. The first four of the Ten Commandments concern worship.[3]

Commandments, however, which came into existence in ancient times, are all very well, but most of us need something more corporeal to which we can respond. Christians believe that this has been provided by the Christ event, Jesus who "became truly human,"[4] God's free gift to us. The new Christians of the first century made the exciting discovery of the sheer gratuitousness of God's act in sending Jesus to them (there was no need for God so to do) and it overwhelmed them.

These essays are concerned with the worship of those churches that belong to the Reformed tradition. Today the term "Reformed" requires explaining in a way that would not have been necessary in former times. During annual visits to the USA I have asked people whose churches are historically in this tradition what it means to them. In many cases they had either not heard of the term or considered it to be of any special relevance for them today.

Basically, "Reformed" describes the tradition that first arose in the sixteenth century as a protest against the belief system, structures, and morality of the church of its day, and a protest for what it believed was the catholic faith.[5] In the English-speaking world, in the aftermath

---

2. The *Shorter Catechism*, together with the *Confession of Faith*, was a product of the Westminster Assembly of Divines, 1643–53, seeking to provide uniformity in doctrine and liturgy for the churches of England, Ireland, and Scotland.

3. Exod 20:1–7.

4. The Nicene Creed. In Thompson, *Stating the Gospel*, 9.

5. The term "Protestant" was first used at the Diet of Speyer in 1529 to describe those princes who protested *for* the catholic faith against what they believed to be Roman error. At the Marburg Colloquy in 1529 a group of Protestant reformers agreed on 14 articles of faith but, fatefully, failed to agree on the fifteenth—"whether the true body and blood of Christ be corporeally present in the bread and wine"—with Luther and Melanchthon taking a different view from Zwingli, Bucer, and Oecolampadius.

of the "great ejection" in the English church of 1662,[6] it developed into several still recognizable forms. These include many within the Church of England,[7] the Church of Scotland (and other Presbyterians), Congregationalists, and Baptists. Methodists came later and some Methodists are more sympathetic to this tradition than to any other—apart from their own! In the USA, the manifestation of denominational traditions has been accompanied by a proliferation of divisions within the traditions themselves, particularly where Baptists are concerned. All of the above owe their existence initially to those critical events of the sixteenth century, and this much they have in common.

The traditional nature of Reformed worship essentially reflected the basis of Reformed teaching (theology) which stresses the sovereignty and holiness of God in Trinity, the centrality of God in the life of the individual and in the life of the world—God first. We do not have a monopoly on this over against other Christians, but we have a particular obligation to affirm this principle boldly by what we say and do in our liturgy. That we are not doing it as well as we should is the main reason why I wrote the book that bears the same title as this essay.

The aforementioned Westminster *Shorter Catechism* (finally approved by the English Parliament in 1648) stressed unequivocally the need to acknowledge God's sovereignty over all, but this doctrine, especially as it has been expressed in the Calvinist-Reformed tradition, has been attacked with some justification from various directions. Some feminist theologians have done so, as have Latin-American Roman Catholic liberation theologians like Leonardo Boff and mainline Protestant scholars such as Jürgen Moltmann. Behind these criticisms lie the old familiar objections that this doctrine robs human beings of

---

This proved to be the beginning of the distinction, and eventually the breach, between the Lutheran and the Reformed streams of Protestantism.

6. The Act of Uniformity of 1662, as well as commanding the use of the *Book of Common Prayer* in the public worship of the Church of England, required of those ministers not episcopally ordained re-ordination by a bishop. It was decreed that those ministers who did not conform by St Bartholomew's Day (24 August) would be deprived of their livings. Upwards of 2,000 ministers, until then ministers in the Church of England, resigned. Among the effects of this "great ejection" was the addition of a significant number of university educated Presbyterian ministers to the ranks of English Dissent—principally, until this point, consisting of Baptists and Congregationalists—and the creation of what soon came to be known as "Nonconformist churches."

7. And other churches of the Anglican Communion, sometimes called "Episcopal"—notably in Scotland and the USA.

both freedom and responsibility and, despite all protests to the contrary, makes God responsible for evil and all the bad things that happen in our individual lives and in the world around us. Yet others have added a new dimension saying that the sovereignty of God presupposes a hierarchical, patriarchal understanding of God that leads to all sorts of misuse of human power.

Now it must be conceded that the traditional Reformed doctrine of the sovereignty of God is indeed subject to some of the more recent criticisms of it. But I believe that if we can challenge effectively this old and speculative doctrine once and for all, we then have the space to make room for a genuinely trinitarian understanding of it, one which would not detract in any way from the sense of the holiness and majesty of the Almighty, that sense of awe which should condition the manner in which we approach together the throne of grace Sunday by Sunday. This would be good news both for people who long for a God who cares enough to be present in the depths of their personal and collective suffering to share it, and for those who also long for a God who is powerful enough to liberate them from every social, political, and ecclesiastical system that oppresses and dehumanizes. Julian Templeton's essay in this volume challenges the criticism that the doctrine of the Trinity is inherently patriarchal by arguing that the mutual giving and receiving of Father, Son, and Holy Spirit is the mode of trinitarian communion to which we are opened in worship. This trinitarian communion has the power to liberate from all forms of oppression.

But whilst it is right and proper to continue to value the intention of the *Shorter Catechism*'s statement, it is helpful when Reformed churches, under the promised guidance of the Holy Spirit, produce updates on it (and there have been many in our tradition). One example in recent years is the statement in the *Directory of Worship* of the Presbyterian Church (USA):

> Christian worship joyfully ascribes all praise and honor, glory and power to the triune God. In worship the people of God acknowledge God present in the world and in their lives. As they respond to God's claim and redemptive action in Jesus Christ, believers are transformed and renewed. In worship the faithful offer themselves to God and are equipped for God's service in the world.

Perhaps it is a little lacking in overt reference to the work of the Holy Spirit but it is certainly implied. At least it provides a gentler introduction than the route taken by the Westminster divines, but one that still encourages an attitude of reverence in our corporate and individual stance before God. And it is this emphasis that seems to be lacking in much Reformed worship today.

According to the great Reformer John Calvin, "Such is pure and genuine religion, namely, confidence in God coupled with serious fear—fear, which both includes in it willing reverence, and brings along with it such legitimate worship as is prescribed by the law."[8] Worship, in other words, should be dignified and reverent, but it does not necessarily achieve these qualities through elaborate ceremonies or complex liturgies, which have not normally been the custom in churches of the Reformation. In fact Calvin believed that, "On all hands there is abundance of ostentatious ceremonies, but sincerity of heart is rare."[9] I would quibble with him to an extent when I think of some devout Roman Catholic friends for whom "complex" liturgies, even those of a Tridentine flavor, are no barrier to their sincerity of heart and to a deep spirituality, and which, in fact, seem to help enhance these dispositions. But Calvin's overall strictures do not imply that Reformed worship has no room for joy or emotion, as many critics have been quick to imply. They have simply not read their Calvin closely enough on this score. He knew that joy, along with a full range of emotions such as grief, anger, desire, hope, and fear, should be a part of worship, though of course not attempting to include them all in one service.

I was baptized in the Church of Scotland where my father was a parish minister before coming to England into the then Presbyterian Church of England.[10] The worship in those churches was very traditional and, yes, bordered on the austere. But I recognize this much. The worship to which I was exposed (sometimes unwillingly) awoke within me a love for God that the slings and arrows of outrageous fortune—never mind chronic ennui—have yet to undo. There was an unselfconscious authenticity in the lives of the people who taught me the rudiments of the faith, and in the solemn, simple sacredness of the worship itself. When we sang "Holy, holy, holy, Lord God Almighty" at the beginning

8. Calvin, *Institutes* Book 1, Chapter 2, Section 2, hereafter cited as *Institutes* 1.2.2.

9. Ibid.

10. Since 1972, part of the URC.

of a service, I now know it was not so I could sing what I meant, but so I could learn to mean what I sang. God was entirely real and worship was a serious business: that much was sure. The sanctuary was no place for shenanigans, frivolity, and flaky humor. The minister did not joke his way through lengthy sermons, though at times there was laughter, good, hearty, and spontaneous laughter. Children were not dismissible props for adults in the pagan act of comic relief we came to call the "children's address." In fact, the strict order to "sit still and listen" was a way of taking children quite seriously, and so respecting them. I imbibed the notion that every service of Holy Communion ought to be a serious venture, demanding self-examination and worthy of our very best attention and response. For here was holiness in action, even if in Scotland the main action (perversely) was not eating and drinking at all, but the awkward dance-macabre of dark-suited elders "distributing the elements."

St Paul wrote to the Corinthians, "All things should be done decently and in order . . . for God is a God not of disorder but of peace."[11] This comes at the end of a homily on worship. In a day when the ministry of Word and sacrament had not emerged in any set form, Paul recognized the importance of the contributions to worship from the whole people of God. These covered a very wide spectrum, involving both speaking in tongues, and more measured offerings. All were welcome as contributions, but the apostle was concerned that things did not get out of hand. Disciplined control, even decorum, was vital if things were not to slip into chaos, thereby threatening the task of building up the fellowship in love.

All worship needs to be embodied in form and, as William Maxwell wrote many years ago, to suppose that the choice lies between form and no form is to imagine a false antithesis, "Form there must always be; and the choice is between various kinds and qualities of form. To eliminate form from worship, all words and acts would require to be eliminated."[12]

Calvin and Luther, and most of the other Reformers, would have agreed with that sentiment. It is true that often the acts of worship in the Protestant traditions have been disparaged by others of a more overtly liturgical persuasion as being shapeless "hymn sandwiches," but such criticism is unfair.

11. 1 Cor 14:40 NRSV.

12. Maxwell, *Concerning Worship*, 40.

Many of our services commenced, and some still do, with the call to worship, usually incorporating a scriptural injunction focusing on the sovereignty and majesty of God. This was followed by a hymn, appropriately one of adoration and praise. After this introduction came the first prayer which continued the theme of adoration. The cumulative acknowledgement of the holiness and sovereignty of God then served by comparison to remind the people of the frailty and sinfulness of our nature. Thus the mood of adoration phased into confession, followed by the pronouncing of the gospel word of pardon.[13] This section concluded with an invocation of the Holy Spirit, praying that the Spirit's presence would now enable the congregation to make a fitting offering of their worship at the throne of grace and renew them in body, mind, and spirit.

Thereafter the first Scripture lesson was read, usually a passage from the Old Testament. This was a reminder that our roots go back long before Christ, to the time of Abraham and Isaac and Jeremiah and David and to many others among whom God was also at work. In the early Christian writings and those of the Reformers it is quite striking how the way in which the great figures in the history of Israel, Abraham and Moses, David and Elijah, seem to be alive within the memory of the church, and Reformed worship at its best has often made a strong contribution in helping to maintain that memory. It was Calvin who opposed the then traditional and commonly accepted assumption of the rejection of Israel. It must be a matter of some concern today that there is a tendency in not a few of our churches to dispense with the reading from the Hebrew Scriptures altogether.

After the first reading a psalm was sung, usually of a metrical kind. Ancient liturgical tradition called it the "gradual." The word comes from the Latin *gradus* meaning a "step" and has its origin in being sung from the altar steps. It also represented a step-like progression from the old covenant to the world of the new and so readings from the Epistle and the Gospel followed. Another hymn would be sung and, thereafter, prayers of thanksgiving and intercession offered. (In modern times there has been a commendable move to place such prayers after the sermon,

---

13. But a good case can be made for placing the confession later in the service, "Penitential rites . . . often make more sense after God's Word is read and interpreted and the congregation know for what omissions and commissions confession is needed." White, *Introduction to Christian Worship*, 142.

especially if the service is not one which concludes with a celebration of the sacrament of Communion).

Probably at this stage the offering would be taken, though we have never quite got this one right and often confuse the two terms of "offering" and "offertory"—the latter refers to the bringing up of the bread and wine to the altar or the holy table at the Eucharist together with the gifts of money from the people, the former should only be to describe the gifts of money. The dedication of the latter would follow, sometimes accompanied by the singing of a doxology such as "Praise God from whom all blessings flow" to the tune *Old Hundredth*, a melody from the *Genevan Psalter* of 1551. Then, after a hymn invoking the presence of the Holy Spirit, the sermon, the preaching of the Word, followed. This, for many, was the high spot of the service. For others it was something which had to be stoically endured. This would not be a miserable ten-minute homily but an event which could last for at least half an hour. In some parts of Scotland in the old days some congregations would think themselves short-changed if it took less than an hour! Of course, thank goodness, this could not be replicated today. If it were to be attempted, our numbers would be even less than they are now. This, however, does not mean that the sermon is of less importance. The preaching of the Word was of fundamental importance in the eyes of the Reformers and so it should be in ours.

Leander Keck, the former Dean at Yale Divinity School, begins his book *The Bible in the Pulpit*, with this paragraph:

> Every renewal of Christianity has been accompanied by a renewal of preaching. Each renewal of preaching, in turn, has rediscovered biblical preaching. Nineteen centuries of experience suggests clearly that unless there is a recovery of biblical preaching, the dissipation of the Christian faith will continue.[14]

He states categorically, "Unless biblical preaching is recovered, the church as a whole will continue to suffer from amnesia."[15] He is not advocating a preaching based on a literalist interpretation of the biblical texts but a hermeneutic approach to it as divine address and as the book of the church. Such a recovery cannot take place without a wrestling with the texts week-by-week. The preacher is called upon to contend with the

14. Keck, *The Bible in the Pulpit*, 11.
15. Ibid., 32.

Bible story, the church's story, and his or her own personal story, as he or she struggles to proclaim God's gracious and judging Word Sunday by Sunday. Anything less is to forget that although the preaching of the Word was not a sacrament to the Reformers, it had a sacramental efficacy, even one that could be independent of the quality of the preaching or of the character of the preacher. They were certainly not Donatists in this respect!

All of the above is not to advocate a return to the lengthy sermon, one that took up time out of all proportion to the rest of the service. But it is to plead for the abolishing of such things as PowerPoint presentations in the sanctuary, which, although having a place in Bible study and catechism, can never be substitutes for the proclaimed and prophetic Word.

Equally irritating is the ubiquitous habit of "theme" preaching. I groan, and not always inwardly, when I enter a church today on either side of the Atlantic, and see at the head of the bulletin sheet that "the theme today" is such and such. It does not take long, by noting the printed lessons and hymns, to work out in advance the predictable course the service will take. Straight away one's expectations are narrowed, lessened by the awareness of the theme, and the element of surprise, which can often strike an awakening chord (sometimes literally!) during an expository sermon that begins with a text, will be absent. The same applies to the largely American custom of sermon titles that are often published in Saturday's local paper, giving an even longer time for the potential worshipper to work out what will be going on and to decide whether or not to give it a miss. This, of course, is the opposite of the intention.

Professor James Stewart was a much-admired Scottish preacher in the second half of the twentieth century. I recall that somewhere he describes how, when he began his ministry as a young man in Scotland, he would sit down each Monday morning in his study and say to himself, "What shall I preach on next Sunday?" He would then think of a subject or theme, perhaps "peace" or "forgiveness" or "justice" or the like, and then set to with a will. But after a few months he discovered that he was running out of subjects and themes. Only then did he begin to take seriously his theological college training and returned to the Scriptures as his starting point. Very soon it came as a pleasant surprise that he could now preach the following Sunday on peace and, with a different text, return to another aspect of it on the next Sunday if he had a mind so to do.

Sermons arising out of the Word of God, speaking through the Scriptures, are open-ended in a way that it is much more difficult for a theme to be. The effect of a true sermon is meant to extend beyond its actual delivery; the preaching enterprise is unfinished business as it feeds from the Scriptures into (ideally) the sacrament of Communion, all three elements being of equal significance when it comes to the business of Christian formation. When the church is careless of form and order, unnecessary distractions enter in and the descent into kitsch is close at hand.[16] At least many of our churches today within the Reformed tradition do make use of the *Revised Common Lectionary.*

I have not mentioned the place of the sacrament of Communion in worship, but I am with Calvin who strongly advocated a weekly celebration of the same, conjoined with the preaching of the Word. I have not dealt further with this important matter because David Thompson takes it up in his contribution to these pages.

But all that I have written so far about re-forming Reformed worship has not taken into account the existence of a growing number of places of worship where a more informal and consumer-friendly style of worship attracts many of those for whom the more formal worship in the mainline churches has not the same appeal. Charismatic and different ethnic groups and evangelical fellowships find us boring and irrelevant. In the United States the so-called "Praise and Worship" phenomenon has become one of the dominant modes of expression within evangelical circles, from conservative Presbyterians to low-church independent congregations. I owe the following observation to Dr D. G. Hart of Westminster Theological Seminary in California. He writes, "What characterizes this style of worship is the praise song ('four words, three notes, and two hours') with its mantra-like repetition of phrases from Scripture, displayed using an overhead projector or video monitor (for those churches with bigger budgets), and accompanied by the standard pieces in a rock band."[17]

A little harsh perhaps and any agreement with Dr Hart could smack of sour grapes from those of us who, week in and week out, minister to dwindling congregations. But he makes a strong case when he states that Praise and Worship services "are part of a self-conscious effort to attract

16. The dictionary defines kitsch as the work in any of the arts that is pretentious and inferior or in bad taste.

17. Hart, *Recovering Mother Kirk*, 82.

a larger market for the church . . . [but] while evangelicalism may have a large market share, its consumer satisfaction may also be low, especially if it deceives people into thinking they have really worshipped God when they have actually been worshipping their emotions."[18]

What are we to make of this phenomenon? I suggest that we have to keep our nerve, hold firmly to our Reformed principles and from them demonstrate in action the liturgical practices that arise naturally from them. But there has been an attempt in recent years in the USA on the part of our churches to have the best of both worlds, that is, the holding of a balance between the formal and the informal. It is, however, mainly recognized that these elements cannot be held together in the same service.

So it is that many a Protestant church's notice board advertises alongside the traditional service that a contemporary service will take place either earlier or later than the former. I have attended several of these so-called contemporary acts of worship, usually in churches where I was to preach afterwards at the main service of the day. There can be no denying the enthusiasm and sincerity of those taking part, mainly young people of course. But worship of a trinitarian emphasis is missing, and is usually focused exclusively on the second person of the Trinity accompanied by catchy songs of a very dubious theology. The majority of those in attendance would not think of the main service as any kind of alternative, and herein lies the problem. How can they be encouraged to advance from what St Paul would call the milk stage to that which provides a more meaty diet? To this end it is essential that there is sensitive, but not too intrusive, oversight on the part of ministers and elders. Other members of the congregation, for whom a contemporary service is not exactly to their liking, should be encouraged to attend from time to time. Personal relationships are all important if there is to be any movement to encourage the young to experience a fuller form of worship that is Reformed worship at its most authentic. Aye—there's the rub! We have to put our own house in order first.

Hughes Oliphant Old, in his study of worship, ends with a reflection about mainline Presbyterian worship that applies well to what has transpired in contemporary evangelical circles. "In our evangelistic zeal, we are looking for programs that will attract people. We think we have to put honey on the lip of the bitter cup of salvation. It is the story of the

18. Ibid., 88.

wedding of Cana all over again but with this difference. At the crucial moment when the wine failed, we took matters into our own hands and used those five stone jars to mix up a batch of Kool-Aid instead."[19]

Commenting on this, Hart writes, "Such is the state of affairs in contemporary evangelical worship. The thin and artificial juice of popular culture has replaced the finely aged and well-crafted drink of the church through the ages. Aside from the merits of the instant drink, it is hardly what you would expect defenders of tradition and the family to serve at a wedding or the banquet supper of our Lord. Yet just as evangelicals in the nineteenth century substituted Welches for red wine, so a century later they have exchanged the superficial and trivial for the rich forms and elements of historic Protestant worship."[20]

Of course Oliphant and Hart mainly had in their sights the big evangelical occasion associated with the mushrooming mega-churches, but that is the only alternative that seems attractive and available to those who have so far been fed on a batch of Kool-Aid in their local churches, and who may begin to look elsewhere for better and bigger experiences. It is a far cry from C. S. Lewis' legitimate description of a true worship service, "The perfect church service would be the one we were almost unaware of; our attention would have been on God. But every novelty prevents this. It fixes our attention on the service itself; and thinking about worship is a different thing from worshipping. ''Tis mad idolatry that makes the service greater than the god'. A still worse thing may happen. Novelty may fix our attention not even on the service but on the celebrant."[21]

But even if it is agreed that we in the churches of the Reformed tradition need to "shape up" when it comes to our liturgical practices, an even greater priority is to get our ecclesiology right, that is our understanding of the nature of the church within which our worship takes place. In this respect we have much to learn once again from our great Father of the Reformation, John Calvin. Quoting St Cyprian, he famously insisted that, "You cannot have God for your Father unless you have the church for your Mother." The church, as he understood it, is a divine institution and not a human contrivance and, theologically understood, the church is part of the divine economy of salvation. This,

---

19. Old, *Worship That is Reformed according to Scripture*, 177.
20. Hart, op cit, 89.
21. Lewis, *Letters to Malcolm*, 4–5.

he claimed, is evident in the pages of the New Testament itself. There, the church is neither an expedience, nor an aggregate of the convinced who, by an act of will, subsequently decide to meet together for mutual help and encouragement.

To be a Christian is to be incorporated into Christ's body, the church; to be incorporated into Christ's body is to be baptized; to be baptized is to belong to Christ; to have been baptized is to be in his body; and to be in his body is to be a Christian.[22]

There is a significant ecclesiology at work here and many Protestants have lost the plot. The ecclesiology we have lost certainly makes space for the full flourishing of the kind of personal relationship to Christ that many evangelical Protestants prize, but it is a relationship—and no other kind is conceivable in the New Testament—that entails a socially-realized incorporation into that body, the church. It is not that social relations are "added" onto a primary relation, it is that our relation to *Jesus* theologically entails social relations (and vice versa). Michael Ramsey, the former Archbishop of Canterbury, wrote, "It is never true to say that separate persons are united to Christ, and then combine to form the church; for to believe in Christ is to believe in One whose Body is part of himself and whose people are his own humanity, and to be joined to Christ is to be joined to Christ-in-his-Body."[23] That is why, in the New Testament, a Christian life lived outside the church is inconceivable; it is because our relation to Christ simply *is* the socially embedded form of life that is the church. It's a form of life in which, to borrow some felicitous sentences of William Temple, "The goal is neither richness of individuality without recognition of the claims of fellowship, nor width of fellowship established between units that have little depth of individuality; the goal is individuality in fellowship where each term is heightened to the maximum."[24] With the loss of our ecclesiology, in both theory and practice, comes a dreadful amnesia. We have forgotten what the church is for and why. Our chief problem is not that the world treats the Protestant church as useless: our chief problem is that some Protestants treat it as useless. For if we think we don't need the church

---

22. If that reasoning sounds "circular" it is meant to be so. The philosopher Edward Caird used to say there's nothing wrong with arguing in a circle provided the circle is big enough.

23. Ramsey, *The Gospel and the Catholic Church*, 36.

24. Temple, *Nature, Man and God*, 449.

and its inherited forms of worship and life, in order to relate to God through Jesus Christ—which is another way of saying that I have no need of *you* or *anyone else* in my relation to the mystery that transcends and enfolds my life—then we are liable to treat the church as something useless the moment it ceases to meet my needs, fails to underwrite my religious aesthetic, refuses to baptize my moral and doctrinal prejudices (or my grandchildren, or whatever I hold most dear), or simply offends my world-view.

So I am suggesting that simply to attempt to reform only our worship in accordance with Reformed ideals is not enough. Such must go hand in hand with the recovery of a true Reformed doctrine of the church. For some Christians the grace of God in Christ is given to rescue us from a fallen world. The world is presented as sinful, lacking in grace, and the church is some kind of ghetto from the world. "The world is not my home; I am just passing through," as the Christian rock artist Larry Norman used to sing. This view affects one's understanding of worship. If the world were evil and things of the world essentially bad for us then the use of the things of the world in worship would surely be a distraction or even a temptation. The Reformed have seen this in part of their liturgical history, with austere churches, no color, no candles, no signs, no symbols. In fact, of course, such churches were highly symbolic, symbolic of a view of the world and of salvation that was "rescue from the world." If, however, the Reformed seeks to be truly *Re-formed*, it should attempt to rediscover a thoroughly sacramental view of life. Those central doctrines of Incarnation and Resurrection come to the fore in the apostle's words, "God was in Christ reconciling the world to himself"[25] and the spiritual is not seen as that which sets us free from the world but rather animates the world, as in Genesis, "The Lord God formed man from the dust of the ground, and breathed into his nostrils the breath of life: and the man became a living being."[26] It is the animation of the material, making material things really real, as it were, that is the basis of a properly Reformed spirituality, worship, and a true understanding of the nature and purpose of the church.[27]

25. 2 Cor 5:19 NRSV.

26. Gen 2:7 NRSV.

27. I am indebted here to Keith Riglin's unpublished lectures, "Baptism, Eucharist and Ministry: Sacraments of Salvation," Summer Programme in Theology, University of Oxford, 1999. See Morgan and Strudwick, *The Way of Salvation*, 63–88.

It is not the loss of individual faith and a commitment that causes the church *per se* to drift and decline; rather, it is the decline of an ecclesial form of life that makes individual faith and commitment more and more impossible. If so, then the reforming and regeneration of Protestant churches cannot come *just* by revising our beliefs and practices into bite-sized morsels that can be palatably swallowed by progressive moderns (a liberal strategy); nor by hectoring the gullible into more muscular belief in "six impossible things before breakfast" (a conservative strategy). No, renewal will come, if ever it does come, by re-invigorating the life of the body and re-vivifying those rituals, practices and skills by which the body is constituted; that social matrix, the church, without which individual belief and practice are impossible.

What I have learnt from one or two great teachers, including a good friend of many years, is this: orthodox Christian faith, and the religious apparatus through which this faith lives, is not a mode of certainty, not a truth we possess and own, nor a technique for controlling and re-engineering the world, not even that piece of the world I identify as myself, this body, this person. Orthodox Christian faith (that of the whole church and not simply our little part of it) is, rather, openness to transcendence, to mystery (openness in heart, mind and will, each one). Its intellectual expression, in the first instance, is not one of certainty at all, but trembling and hesitation in the face of mystery, and therefore not just hesitation but *humility.* Indeed our "chief and highest end is to glorify God, and fully to enjoy God for ever."

3

Looking Back: A Historical Overview of Reformed Worship

BY DAVID CORNICK

THE REFORMED MOVEMENT WAS polyphonous, maybe even ca-cophonous, from its birth. What we call "the Reformation" for convenience was in fact a mosaic of reformations across the city-states and towns of what is now Germany and Switzerland. Each locality was shaped by subtly different socio-economic and political forces, the experience of individuals before God and their neighbors, and the interchange of theological and ecclesiological ideas within a community of discourse that transcended political boundaries. Ideas and practices formed in one place rarely survived export to another intact – they were amended and molded into different contexts. So it was that Bucer's *Kirchenpfleger* became Calvin's rather different *Elders*, and Bucer fused Schwarz's 1524 German Mass and Zwingli's pattern of worship to produce a uniquely Strassbourgian blend in 1539. Whilst we may find unifying themes in the early history of Reformed worship—the importance of Scripture, or the desirability of all communicating in both bread and wine, or a wariness of the visual—we will discover neither theological nor liturgical uniformity. But it is the themes that are significant, for they are evidence of a theology which was exploring the contours of a transcendent God in a land where the common spiritual currency was immanence, the first stirring of a process which would eventually re-frame Western European culture. In the anarchic excitement of the early 1520s, those ideas surfaced without regard for later distinctions between traditions. Let me begin, then, with two lesser-known reformers: Andreas Karlstadt and Leo Judt.

KARLSTADT AND JUDT

In 1520 Elector Frederick of Saxony wisely removed Luther from cir-
culation and shut him up in the Wartburg, leaving a power vacuum in
Wittenberg, which was filled (amongst others) by Andreas Karlstadt, a
brave man who had stood beside Luther in the years when the whole
world stood against them. Whilst he lacked Luther's theological stature,
he shared his integrity. Yet with Luther gone, there was no one to apply
the brakes, and Karlstadt tumbled helter-skelter into reform. In the autumn of 1521 his polemical edge was sharpened in a series of pamphlets
on clerical marriage, vows, and communion in both kinds. Then, on
Christmas Day 1521, in defiance of the civic authorities, he celebrated
a simple Communion service with no sacrificial language and no vest-
ments, offering the people both bread and wine. The following day this
middle-aged academic announced his engagement to fifteen year old
Anna von Mochau, the none-too-pretty daughter of a poor gentleman,
and a fortnight later secured his place in history by becoming the first
reformer to marry.[1] Luther smartly distanced himself from his col-
league, although the friendship between them survived. Karlstadt lacked
Luther's liturgical moderation. He was driven by the conviction that the
guidance of Scripture was the prime liturgical principle, and he found
there what he believed to be an unquestionable denunciation of images
in the ten commandments, "You shall not make for yourself an idol,
whether in the form of anything that is in the heaven above, or that is
on the earth beneath, or that which is in the water under the earth. You
shall not bow down to them or worship them: for I the Lord your God
am a jealous God . . ."[2] "I say to you . . . ," Karlstadt commented in his *On
the abolition of images* (1522), "that God has forbidden images with no
less diligence than killing, stealing, adultery, and the like."[3]

A year later, preaching in *St. Peterskirche* in Zurich, across the river
from Zwingli's *Grossmünster*, Leo Judt explored the same theme. Judt
was a distinguished Hebraist, and he noticed what the Western church
had largely forgotten, namely that there were two ways of ordering the
Ten Commandments. Western Christians, on the authority of Augustine
and others, treated the condemnation of idolatry as a sub-clause of the

1. See Rupp, *Patterns of Reformation*, 49–149.
2. Exod 20:2 NRSV.
3. Eire, *War Against the Idols*, 58.

first commandment, but Judaism and the Eastern church treated it as a separate commandment, which is why the icon emerged as a two-dimensional art form. The mood of the Swiss reformations was set. These smoldering academic coals would soon break into iconoclastic fire. The commandments were re-numbered.

Zwingli picked up the theme in his preaching at the *Grossmünster*, and small-scale image breaking erupted. The city council decided to deal with the rising tensions by a public disputation, the Second Zurich Disputation of October 1523, which ended by condemning the Mass and images. Not until the following June did the council call for images to be removed from the city's churches. Then, in two weeks the ". . . statues, paintings, murals, altar decorations, votive lamps, and carved choir stalls" that had shaped the spirituality of centuries were swept away to be replaced by white-washed walls, a liturgy centered on the reading of Scripture and preaching and a plain wooden table around which the Lord's Supper was celebrated.[4] Here there were no distractions for the eye, and the ear became the doorway into the invisible world where the holy and transcendent God dwelt.

Back in Wittenberg, Luther, remained strenuous in his defense of images, and turned a deaf ear to the cogency of Judt's argument. That had two results. First, it was to mean that Roman Catholics and Lutherans would number the Ten Commandments in the Augustinian way, and all other Protestants follow the Eastern Orthodox tradition. Second, it was a parting of the ways between Luther and the Swiss, exacerbated by their later profound disagreement about the Eucharist, which not even Calvin could heal. Artistically, architecturally, liturgically, the reforming river was now to flow in two diverging streams, Lutheran and Reformed.

Art has such a high, almost sacred, value in our society that it is almost impossible to think ourselves into the mind-set of such an aniconic theology, but it is important to do so, for if we do not, we will fail to appreciate the essential dynamics of Reformed worship. Karlstadt, Judt, Zwingli, and Calvin were not uncultured ruffians, but the cream of the educated humanist elite. Their objection was not to art—Calvin in particular gives a spirited defense of civic and domestic art in the *Institutes*. It was rather the use of art in church, as they saw it in defiance of the very words of God himself: that was problematic. Karlstadt captured it beautifully when he wrote, ". . . all the pictures on earth put together

---

4. See Eire, op. cit., 83.

cannot give you one tiny sigh towards God." The mystery, majesty, and wonder of God was so far beyond the reach of the intellect, the scope of the emotions and the depth of human imagination, that even the finest art was rendered inarticulate and incapable. The unbridgeable gap between God and humanity could only be bridged by God's love and grace, made manifest in Christ, witnessed in Scripture, made real in preaching and sacraments. As Karlstadt put it, "The Word of God is spiritual, and it alone is useful to the believer."[5]

THE REFORMATION'S REVOLUTION

This was shocking radicalism in the early decades of the sixteenth century, where the whole spiritual and liturgical economy was constructed around the immanence of God which crackled with the electricity of holiness in the sacraments of the church, the shrines and relics of the saints, and the eucharistic host; a veritable web of holy places and things that linked heaven and earth, and made God real in the everyday. The collapse of that economy had, of course, been foreshadowed in the droll, dry pen of that stern critic of Cambridge beer, Erasmus of Rotterdam. But it was his humanist children who rolled it out in liturgical reality.

It was first a re-ordering of time, of the day, the week, the cycles of the seasons and the year. Late medieval time was Christian time, working through a cycle that began with Advent, and passed through Christmastide, Lent, Easter, Pentecost, Trinity, and Corpus Christi. Whilst some social historians have argued that this divided the year into "ritualistic" and "secular" halves, Eamon Duffy is surely right when he points out that in the summer the deficit of propers was compensated for by the number of festivals which fell in the summer and autumn—St Thomas Becket, St Margaret, St James the Apostle, and St Anne in July, the Transfiguration, the Holy Name of Jesus, the Beheading of John the Baptist, and above all the Assumption in August, the birth of Our Lady, Holy Cross, the feast of the Apostle Matthew, and Michaelmas in September, Luke and Simon and Jude in October, and then All Saints and All Souls in November, to say nothing of the celebrations of local saints like Hugh of Lincoln, and Edmund, King and Martyr. The result, as he notes, was a "... close interweaving of the

5. Ibid., 59.

church's calendar with divisions and uses of time which in essence had little to do with the Christian year."[6]

All of that was laid to one side. In the Reformed understanding of time, the Christological framework of the year is retained—Easter, Ascension, Pentecost, Christmas—and left in its simple majesty. The barnacles of tradition, the Marian festivals and the feasts of the saints, and such johnny-come-lately sideshows as Corpus Christi, are cleaned away. What replaces it is a cycle of weekly holy-days (holidays)—Sunday was a full holiday, Wednesday a partial one. Far from being a secularizing of time, this is a radical re-sacralizing of time, and it is theologically determined.

A REFORMED UNDERSTANDING OF WORSHIP

The Reformed believed that God had appointed his trysting place where he would meet with humanity: Jesus Christ the Word made flesh, made sacramentally present through the preaching of the Word and the Lord's Supper. In Book One of the *Institutes* Calvin argues that there are two sources of knowledge about the world: knowledge of God and knowledge of ourselves.[7] Like all medieval theologians, he believed that human nature was deeply flawed, so the journey inwards was a non-starter, as it continued to be until Schleiermacher. If true knowledge was the goal, the only reliable methodology was to know God in the way God had appointed, discerned in Scripture through the guidance of the Spirit, and experienced through union with Jesus Christ. That experience of re-creation enabled the individual to live with vocational delight in the world, which was truly the theatre of God's glory. It was precisely there, in the world, that they would encounter God, but only after worship on Sunday and Wednesday, and daily Bible reading, had provided the correct methodological spectacles with which to see God, whose providential handwriting was to be discerned in the exquisite rationality of the world. Worship enabled Reformed people to play their part in the theatre of God's glory. It made their time God's time, and their space God's space.

The precise forms of early Reformed liturgies were forged by the interaction of theology, humanism, and tradition. Innovative, exciting Biblical theology (at least in the 1520s) was woven into a social struc-

6. Duffy, *The Stripping of the Altars*, 46–48.
7. See Calvin, *Institutes*, 1.1.1.

ture that respected scholarship and held on tenaciously to traditional practices. That is why Reformed worship can be mistaken for an Open University broadcast, and why Reformed eucharistic celebration varies from the quarterly to the monthly. Despite clear and cogent theological arguments for the equality of Word and sacrament, despite even Calvin's persuasiveness, some reformers and most secular authorities stuck to the established pattern, behind which lies the very un-Reformed fear of unworthy reception. In *Action or Use of the Lord's Supper* (1525) Zwingli argued that Communion should be celebrated four times a year: Christmas, Easter, Pentecost, and on the festival of Zurich's patron saints, Felix and Regula (11 September). The service was simple, dramatic, and austere, and it rapidly became the pattern for Zurich's quarterly celebrations. A table was set up in the nave, and the ministers in black academic gowns stood behind it facing the people as fellow believers, not priests. All recited the Gloria, the Creed, and Psalm 113. The people were then exhorted to receive the gifts of God properly, and prayer for faith followed. The words of the institution were then read and a period of silence was kept. Then the bread and wine were distributed, the people passing the elements to each other whilst remaining seated whilst one of the ministers read John 13. Zwingli had effectively surgically removed the Eucharist from the ministry of the Word. Later in 1525 he set out the "normal" Sunday service of the Word. It drew on Ulrich Surgant's service of *pronus* or *pronaus*, based on the medieval service of prone from his *Manuale Curatorum* (1502). It was intended to be a separate preaching service before Mass.[8] The structure was:

> Announcement of Text
> Lord's Prayer
> Ave Maria
> Sermon
> Bidding Prayer and Remembrance of the Departed
> Lord's Prayer
> Ave Maria
> Apostles' Creed
> Decalogue
> General Confession
> Absolution

8. Spinks, *From the Lord and "the Best of the Reformed Churches,"* 48.

Zwingli adapted the model, centering on the reading of Scripture and the sermon. There was no music. Interestingly, he preserved a Hail Mary, the commemoration of the dead, and the ending with the confession and pardon because he thought you could not confess until you had heard the promises of the gospel proclaimed in the sermon.[9] His principal innovation was to reject the lectionary, preferring the ancient method of *lectio continua*.

Studies of Reformed worship tend to begin with Calvin, the acceptable face of Reformed liturgy, but they omit Zwingli at their peril. A generation before Calvin, he created a pattern which has been remarkably influential, not least in the separation of the ministry of the Word and the Eucharist, the frequency of celebration, *lectio continua,* and the use of the institution narrative as a warrant. Mercifully, the Reformed movement was pluriform, so that in time Zwinglian raw meat was tenderized by Lutheran spices. Martin Bucer, that most irenic of reformers, was a liturgical craftsman whose work was to have a decisive influence on both Calvin, who worked alongside him in Strasbourg from 1538–41, and Thomas Cranmer who lent him protection in 1548, bringing him to Cambridge as the Regius Professor of Divinity. Scholars have long seen Bucer's hand in the 1549 *Book of Common Prayer*. At the beginning of his time in Strasbourg he followed a Zwinglian liturgical path, but as he sought unity between the Lutheran and Swiss reformations, he began to experiment, blending Diebold Schwarz's 1524 German Mass with Zwinglian patterns, until he finally settled on his 1539 liturgy:

The Liturgy of the Word

From the communion table . . .
"In the name of the Father, Son, and Holy Spirit"
Call to Confession
Prayer of Confession
Word of Comfort [1 Timothy 1:15, or other passage]
Absolution
Psalm or hymn, and sometimes the Gloria in Excelsis
Singing was unaccompanied, led by the Precentor
Prayer for Illumination
Metrical Psalm or Ten Commandments
From the pulpit . . .

---

9. See Rice and Huffstutler, *Reformed Worship*, 30.

The Liturgy of the Table

Celebrated weekly in the Cathedral, monthly elsewhere
From the communion table . . .
Collection of Alms
The Apostles' Creed [sung]
Intercession and Consecration Prayer
    [ending with the Lord's Prayer]
Institution and Fraction
Communion [while psalm is sung]
Post-communion Prayer
Aaronic Benediction[10]

If Zwingli had pushed the theology of the primacy of Scripture to its logical conclusion by separating Word and Eucharist; Bucer restored liturgical sanity by holding Word and sacrament together within the broad historical structure of the Mass. So, even when the sacrament was not celebrated, its form was retained, reminding the faithful that the central act of Christian worship was the Holy Communion. Music was restored through singing, and movement too as the people went forward and gathered around the table to receive. This was to be Calvin's model, "I took the form of Strasbourg, and borrowed the greater part of it."[11] Whilst he was ministering to the French congregation in Strasbourg, he translated Bucer's service into French and introduced a few innovations of his own—such as singing the Decalogue in meter with a Kyrie after each commandment and singing of the Nunc Dimittis after Communion. Back in Geneva in 1542 he produced a simplified version of the rite, *La forme des Prières*. As ever, compromises were necessary with the magistracy—the absolution became an assurance of pardon, the sung Decalogue disappeared as rapidly as it came, and the institution narrative was placed before the prayer of consecration as a Scriptural warrant.[12]

---

10. Meyerhoff, "Pioneer of Reformed worship—Celebrating the 500th Anniversary of Martin Bucer," www.reformedworship.org/magazine/article.cfm?_id=579.

11. Cited in Barkley, *The Worship of the Reformed Church*, 16.

12. See Rice and Huffstutler, op. cit., 34.

Liturgy of the Word

Scripture sentence[13]
Confession of sins
Metrical Psalm
Collect for Illumination
Scripture Lesson

Liturgy of the Faithful

Intercessions
Lord's Prayer
Apostles' Creed (and preparation of the elements)
Scriptural Warrant
Exhortation
Prayer of Consecration
Fraction
Delivery
Communion (psalm sung, or Scripture read)
Post-Communion Prayer
Aaronic blessing

Calvin was, of course, an advocate of weekly Communion, but the city fathers were firm in their dismissal of his pleas. In 1561 he stated plainly, "I have taken care to record publicly that our custom is defective, so that those who come after me may be able to correct it the more freely and easily."[14] Just as in Strasbourg, the service of the Word remains an ante-Communion, a silent reminder of what should be. Just as in Strasbourg, music was cherished, as Calvin used the talents of Louis Bourgeois and Claude Goudimel (Palestrina's teacher) and the poetic ability of Clement Marot to create a psalm-singing people. In Geneva there were four Sunday services. The first, at dawn, was intended for servants and others whose duties would occupy them for the remainder of the day. Its pattern mirrored the main service at eight, so on Sundays when the Lord's Supper was celebrated at eight, it was also celebrated at dawn. The noon service was for children and catechumens. The final preaching service was at three (two in the winter). Calvin normally preached at the

13. Italics indicate material taken from Calvin's Strasbourg rite.
14. Cited in Barkley, op. cit., 20.

eight and the three unless important duties demanded he be elsewhere. Daily preaching services were held throughout the rest of the week, with Wednesday designated especially as a day of prayer. Preaching took the form of *lectio continua*, so there was continual movement through Scripture.

THE WESTMINSTER DIRECTORY

It was, of course, Calvin's pattern that was to determine the structure of Scottish, English, and American Reformed liturgies as the Marian exiles like Knox returned from Geneva to Scotland and England with copies of Calvin's order in their pockets. Yet for all the lack of acknowledgement of Zwingli's radicalism,[15] his influence is there for all to see in what is not done. However, from 1560, when the first General Assembly of the Church of Scotland directed that ". . . the sacraments be ministered after the order of the kirk of Geneva," until 1645 when the *Directory for the Public Worship of God* was produced by the Westminster Assembly in a vain attempt to provide a common pattern for English, Scottish, and Irish worship, it remained normative, and it was to become so again in the twentieth century. Liturgically it is hard to feel much sympathy with the Westminster *Directory*. It was, as Principal Robert Baillie of Glasgow University, one of the Scottish commissioners, observed, a compromise, ". . . one party purposing by the preface to turn the Directory into a straight Liturgie; the other to make it so loose and free, that it should serve for little use."[16] It began as an attempt to Puritanize the *Book of Common Prayer*, but the commissioners were unfortunately clear about what they wanted taken out—private baptisms, kneeling, saints' days, and so forth—but much less clear about what they wanted in. What emerged was in vague harmony with Calvin's order, but much was changed. The *Directory* represented the rise of Independent angst about extempore prayer, and it offered guides and patterns for prayer—didactic, prolix, preachy—and long. The prayer of confession moves from confession to petition to intercession. Baillie commented that it was ". . . a new fancy of the Independents, grounded on no solid reason, and contraire to all the practice of the church, old or late, who divided their prayers into

15. But see Barkley, op. cit., 21. ". . . this understanding of his teaching has left a lasting mark on the worship and practice of all the Reformed churches."

16. Cited in Davies, *Worship and Theology in England: from Andrewes to Baxter and Fox*, 407–8.

small parts, and did not have any one of a disproportionate length."[17] It has been described as the only prayer book in the world that consists of nothing but rubrics. More significantly, it took Reformed worship out of the hands of the people and gave it to the minister. New presbyter was indeed but old priest writ large. Sadly, the *Directory* set the pattern for Scottish and English Free church worship for two centuries. The liturgical heritage of Bucer, Calvin, and Knox was well and truly lost.

PRESBYTERIAN AND CONGREGATIONAL WORSHIP

Whilst there are clear similarities between developments in English and Scottish worship, an historical question emerges at this point. English Presbyterianism drifted gently into Unitarianism, to be re-invigorated in the nineteenth century by exilic Scots. Independency flourished as a by-product of the Evangelical Revival. The fusion of the International Congregational Council with the World Alliance of Reformed Churches in 1970, and the Congregational and Presbyterian union two years later to create the United Reformed Church, can mask the significant differences between those traditions. The index of Sylvester Horne's 1903 *History of the Free Churches* gives short shrift to the Reformation— Luther is mentioned six times, Calvin once and Zwingli not at all. The heritage that was cherished and explored was the radical underground of Cromwellian England.[18] It could be argued that Congregationalism owes little to Geneva except the broad Protestant debt to Calvin's *Institutes*, and the question therefore arises of whether Congregational worship at this period is Reformed worship at all, or something rather different. In his study of the development of Congregational liturgy, Bryan Spinks calls the period 1658–1800 "a period of liturgical obscurity." An account survives from 1723 of morning worship in Isaac Watts' Bury Street Chapel:

> In the morning we begin with singing a psalm, then a short prayer follows to desire the divine presence in all the following parts of worship; after that, about half an hour is spent in the exposition of some portion of Scripture, which is succeeded by singing a psalm or an hymn. After this the minister prays more at large, for all the variety of blessings, spiritual and temporal, for

17. Davies, op. cit., 412.

18. Cornick, "Twentieth-Century Historians of English Protestant Nonconformity," 63–77.

the whole congregation, with confessions of sins, and thanksgiv-
ings for mercies . . . Then a sermon is preached, and the morning
worship concluded with a short prayer and a benediction.

The afternoon was more of the same, minus the first short prayer and
exposition, and with a psalm just after or before the sermon, and once
a month the Lord's Supper was celebrated, following the afternoon sermon in the summer, or at noon in the winter—this separation of Word
and Sacrament being an example of the long arm of Zwingli extending
over the English capital. It should be noted that Anglicanism at this period fared not much better, with mattins and a sermon being the norm,
except in a few cathedrals.

In the sixteenth century Reformed worship re-sacralized time, in
the seventeenth it secularized it. Thanks to Puritanism's excesses the
christological framework of time was gone. Robert Browne described
Christmas, Easter, and Whitsun as ". . . dung . . . received from Baal," so
Sundays were the holy mountains of the year. As Michael Watts wryly
noted, ". . . the Quakers with characteristic iconoclasm opened their
shops on Christmas Day . . ."[19] To counteract the boredom, one assumes.
That said, what survived in this period was the primacy of the Word, the
development of hymnody to accompany and interpret it, and the discovery of an architectural style shaped by the specificity of a Word-centered
liturgy. The meetinghouse was the objective correlative of dissenting social structure, a place for a gathered people to meet together around the
Word, designed so that the Word could be heard and the preacher seen.
A minister-centric liturgy does not mean a passive people. As Michael
Watts points out, Sunday's devotions did not end when the chapel door
closed following the afternoon service. Back home around the hearth
sermons were discussed, dissected, even memorized. It is one of the her-
esies of our age that listening is a passive activity. It is not. For all their
liturgical shortcomings, our eighteenth-century forbears understood
the essential dynamic of Reformed worship— through the Word, God
comes.

This is not the place to explore the links between the Evangelical
Revival and Romanticism, but as Georgian England slowly evolved into
Victorian England, sensibilities and mores shifted, all things medieval
and Gothic became gateways to reality, and the beauty of holiness trans-

19. Watts, *The Dissenters: from the Reformation to the French Revolution*, 312–13. He
also cites the Bury St account there.

formed worship. The Oxford Movement was to exercise a profound influence. In its wake came much that we take for granted: flowers in church, robed choirs, anthems, and candles. That—rather than the rediscovery of the European Reformation—transformed Free church worship in England. A back street chapel will not do when you have ridden the waves of commercial success and are sending your children to Rugby School and are knocking on the doors of the University of Oxford. Nor will the stumbling platitudes of a poorly-educated preacher. Socially and ecclesiastically, Congregationalism came of age in the nineteenth century, and that had liturgical consequences. These liturgical consequences, in turn, had architectural consequences.

TWO EXAMPLES OF ENGLISH CONGREGATIONAL ARCHITECTURE

Two contrasting Congregational buildings offer differing perspectives: Union Chapel, Islington and Mansfield College Chapel, Oxford. James Cubbitt designed Union Chapel in 1876–79. Cubbitt drew his inspiration from the eleventh-century octagonal Santa Fosca in Torcello, Venice, a building that inspired Ruskin almost to rapture in *The Stones of Venice*.[20]

20. Binfield, *The Contexting of a Chapel Architect*, 55.

Interior of Union Chapel, Islington

Union Chapel is an extraordinary building. It is a profoundly Reformed space, designed (as were the Huguenot temples) with the twin aims of hearing and seeing. The acoustics are exceptional, both for the spoken word and music. Every seat is within the preacher's sightline, and every member of the congregation can see the preacher. The relationship between the individual and God made present in Scripture and preaching is at once direct and intensely personal, yet also collective. The rippling flow of pews through the octagonal space forces the congregation to be aware of each other as they sit under the Word and rise to sing their praises. It is protestantly individual, yet as collective as catholicism. Union Chapel was the pulpit of that most cultured of Congregationalists, Henry Allon, a representative of that movement begun by Thomas Binney at the King's Weigh House, London, to set new standards of nonconformist worship. Along with his two singularly gifted organists, H. J. Gauntlett, from 1853 until 1861, and Ebenezer Prout, from 1861 until 1873, Allon encouraged chanted psalmody. He also edited a series of hymnbooks in the 1870s and 80s.[21]

Bryan Spinks' analysis of the Congregational liturgical revival is telling. The adopted heritage was diverse: the Puritanism of the Westminster *Directory*, adaptations of the *Book of Common Prayer* (which had been introduced into Congregationalism by the Countess of Huntingdon), Zwinglian eucharistic theology, the early Fathers. But not until J. S. Whale, Nathaniel Micklem, and the "new Genevans" of the 1930s is there a whiff of Calvin or any serious attempt to rectify the sundering of Word and Supper.

The Victorian re-discovery of Gothic let image back into Reformed space, at least in stained glass windows. Union Chapel had thirty stained glass windows, the gift of a benefactor. Cubbitt had little control of them, but he makes sparing use of images: angels flying in the rose windows above the arcades. His materials were fine: polished granite, Yorkshire stone, encaustic tiles, polished marble, all nicely judged to produce a harmonious effect.

The second building, erected some ten years later, is the chapel of Mansfield College, Oxford, which the German theologian Friedrich Heiler once called "the most catholic place in Oxford."[22] Mansfield is a quiet triumph of Nonconformist Gothic by Basil Champneys. Champneys was an Anglican, the son of a Dean of Lichfield Cathedral. His legacy includes some of the best nineteenth century university build-ings: the Rylands library in Manchester; the Dutch Revival buildings at Newnham College, Cambridge; the old Cambridge Divinity School; and Oxford's Indian Institute. He made Mansfield chapel a symphony of stained glass and statues. Aniconic it is not. The chapel faces north, and the north window represents Christ in glory surrounded by St Paul, the apostles and the great figures of the Old Testament. But more interesting are the east and west windows and the statues between them. Added in 1906 after a benefaction, they are a wonderfully ecumenical collection of the saints of God: representatives of the Greek and Latin church, the medieval church, the Puritan tradition, and the eighteenth century, all looking down on the worshipping congregation.[23]

21. Kaye, Elaine, "Henry Allon."

22. Davies, *Worship and Theology in England: from Newman to Martineau*, 56.

23. Kaye, *Mansfield College*, 80.

Interior of Mansfield College Chapel, Oxford

As a building it is both a cultural and a spiritual statement. Culturally, as has often been acknowledged, it represented the "alternative" world of English Dissent reaching an intellectual and social maturity, becoming part of the Arnoldian dream. Less fully noted is the manner in which it spoke of the quiet confidence of a Reformed tradition able now to present itself as both Reformed and catholic, and unafraid of catholic methodology. The saints are back, around the walls and in the windows, yet not all saints. Of the English Henrician reformation there is not a trace.[24] The building is designed so that the congregation are all within the preacher's eye line, its plan longitudinal. This too is a place for a congregation to be together, a collective in praise. There seems to be one fundamental change, a pulpit placed to one side, with a central communion table. However, the reason was pragmatic and thoroughly Reformed—it was better acoustically. Nonetheless, it was serendipitous, for it anticipated the recovery of balance between Word and sacrament,

24. Binfield, *So Down to Prayers*, 166.

which would be one of central discoveries of the new-Genevan Calvinist revival of the mid twentieth century.

Mansfield College, Oxford. Main Building on left, Chapel on right.

The contrast between those two buildings points to an important principle within the Reformed tradition, the balance between form and freedom, the ability to craft worship around the needs and inclinations of the local congregation. We have always had our oddities. If on the one hand, Zwinglianism rules; then on the other, Geneva can be Rome re-devivus. When Westminster College moved from London to Cambridge in 1899, its church history tutor, John Gibb, moved with it. It would be fair to say he was an unusual Presbyterian minister. In London he preferred the ritualistic glory of St Alban's Church, Holborn to the stately solemnity of Regent Square Presbyterian Church, and in Cambridge was to be found be-surpliced in King's College chapel rather than be-suited in St Columba's Church. "He spoke," said his biographer, "of Rome with veneration, and of Geneva with respect, and of himself as 'a Christian . . .'"[25] Maybe something of his unconventionality rubbed off on one of his pupils, W. E. Orchard.

25. Townsend, *The Mind of John Gibb*, 48.

W. E. ORCHARD

Orchard left Westminster College, Cambridge, in 1904 for St Paul's Presbyterian Church, Enfield, where he established a considerable reputation as a preacher. Socialism, the "New Theology" of R. J. Campbell and a growing interest in Dante, Julian of Norwich, and the Quietist tradition were hallmarks of a questing, exploring ministry that pushed at the edges and sought to re-interpret the gospel for a new century. Catholic practices began to edge into the liturgy and a crucifix appeared at the back of the pulpit. He was a man to be noticed, and sure enough in 1913 a call came from John Hunter's Trinity Church, Glasgow, the jewel in Scottish Congregationalism's crown. He refused. The following year he narrowly failed to gain nomination as the President of Cheshunt College (he is the most interesting President Cheshunt never had), but accepted a call to the King's Weigh House in Mayfair, London. His ministry began on 4 October 1914. To quote his biographer, "The large congregation at the morning service rose to its feet as Orchard, clad in loose cassock, Roman collar, silk surplice, embroidered stole and sanctuary shoes adorned with John Wesley's silver buckles, entered the chancel, followed by the surpliced choir. As he knelt on the marble steps to intone the invocation, it must have been clear that this was the beginning of no ordinary conventional Congregational ministry."[26]

It certainly wasn't. However, Orchard never did anything that was not approved first by the church meeting. A preacher of outstanding power, he was a sought after missioner in Great Britain and the USA. A pacifist of stout conviction, he was also a robust champion of the rights of women in both church and state. Liturgically and devotionally he sought deliberately to ". . . try to embrace all that is best in Protestantism with all that is best in Catholicism . . ."[27] In 1929, towards the end of his ministry there, *The Christian World* printed a report of worship at the Weigh House. Brilliant evangelistic preaching, delivered without a note and nuanced with passion, was followed by a remarkable transformation:

> A curtain was drawn back, and in three minutes all trace of a Congregational church had vanished, and we were gazing at a catholic altar, ablaze with forty candles. A procession of choristers entered the choir from the sacristy, the rear being brought

26. Kaye and Mackenzie, *Orchard*, 54.
27. Ibid.

up by Dr Orchard vested in a splendid garment for the service of "benediction". A consecrated host was taken from the tabernacle, incense was burned before it, the famous hymns, *O Salutaris hostia* and *Tantum ergo* (both in English, were sung), then amidst clouds of incense the host was waved before the people in the form of a cross—and all was over.[28]

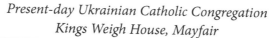

Present-day Ukrainian Catholic Congregation
Kings Weigh House, Mayfair

Orchard's journey ended with reception into the Roman priesthood: for him, at least, a homecoming. Such journeys did not all have to end in Rome. If Orchard is the extreme; the Genevans are the median, reminding the tradition that it is part of the universal church, catholic and Reformed. There were liturgical consequences, but it is hard to image John Whale organizing a service of solemn benediction.

DEVELOPMENTS IN NINETEENTH AND TWENTIETH-CENTURY PRESBYTERIAN WORSHIP

Liturgical scholarship was key to the transformation of Scottish and English Presbyterian worship. The Church Service Society, formed in 1865, exercised leadership and leverage, providing a forum for the study of ancient and modern liturgies, and publishing re-prints of long forgotten

28. Ibid., 86.

Scottish liturgies. Three of its members were responsible for the creation of possibly the most influential prayer book ever produced in Scotland, the *Euchologion* (1867). With generous catholicity, it drew on Calvin's Strasbourg and Genevan liturgies, American German Reformed liturgy, Bishop Jeremy Taylor, the Liturgy of St Basil, the Catholic Apostolic Church, and included prayers by (amongst others) St Augustine, Luther, William Laud, Bright, and Martineau. It was a brave and beautiful book, and it paved the way for the development of both Scottish and English Presbyterian books. Perhaps its most significant impact in England was that it opened the door to the riches of liturgical catholicity for the Free churches in a non-threatening way.

The English Presbyterians eventually broke away from the Westminster *Directory* in the *Revised Westminster Directory* (1898). Any liturgy produced by a denominational committee will be more conservative than a private publication, so comparison with *Euchologion* is unfair. The denomination was deeply divided about it, and it was wisely never sent down to presbyteries for approval. Nonetheless, despite its conservatism, it provided an optional norm for all Presbyterians, which, as Horton Davies points out, was ". . . considerably more than the English Baptists or Congregationalists had achieved."[29] The pattern is familiar:

Order of Service

Invitation to Worship
Prayer of Invocation
Psalm/Hymn
Prayers of Adoration and Confession and Petition for Pardon
Old Testament Lection
Hymn
(Optional children's address)
New Testament Lection
(Optional recitation of the Apostles' Creed)
Prayers of Thanksgiving, Supplication, Intercession and Lord's
    Prayer
Psalm/Hymn
Announcements
(Optional Prayer for Illumination)

---

29. Davies, *Worship and Theology in England: from Newman to Martineau*, 111.

Sermon and brief concluding prayer
Offertory
Psalm/Hymn
Blessing

The Communion Order

Exhortation and fencing of tables
Hymn
Psalm or appropriate passages of Scripture
Prayer of Approach
Eucharistic Prayer (including *epiclesis*, oblation, and optional *Sanctus*)
Distribution
Brief exhortation (optional)
Prayers of Thanksgiving and Intercession for the church militant and remembrance of the faithful departed
Psalm/Hymn
Offering for the poor
Blessing (Heb 13:20–21)

At least in English Presbyterianism, Zwingli lay vanquished. The book paved the way for further revisions in 1921 and 1948. By then, however, Micklem, Whale, Bernard Lord Manning, Carnegie Simpson, and such fine Scottish liturgical scholars as W. D. Maxwell, had reminded Congregationalists and Presbyterians of their continental Reformed heritage, and Reformed worship regained depth and resonance as it reconnected with its Calvinist past. Ironically, sadly, despite the witness of the Churches of Christ, in most places, Word and sacrament are still sundered. Maybe, after all, Zwingli has had the last laugh.

4

What's the Problem with God the Father?

Some Implications of Impersonal References to God in Reformed Liturgy

BY JULIAN TEMPLETON

GOD SPEAKS. GOD IS voluble. God utters the aspirate Word, and the Word creates, makes covenant, instructs by law, proclaims through prophecy, and becomes incarnate. The incarnate Word, Jesus of Nazareth, instructed his followers to pray to God as "Our Father in heaven . . ."[1]—a personal address, striking in its familiarity and intimacy. As creatures of the Word, humans share something of God's volubility and eloquence. For us, words matter. The words that liturgists and leaders of worship use are important because it is by words they indicate the character of the God whom we approach, praise, beseech in prayer, listen to, commune with, and invoke in blessing. It is often by words that we are led into God's presence and sense something of God's glory. In this essay I will explore the implications of the practice of referring to God the Holy Trinity using inclusive language, using a recent liturgy of my denomination as a case study. This will lead into a discussion of the claim made by some feminist theologians that calling God "Father" reinforces patriarchy. I will then discuss whether the doctrine of the Trinity may itself subvert patriarchy. This will be followed by an examination of the gendered nature of language, and by a discussion of the tension

---

1. See Matt 6:9.

43

between allegiance to family and allegiance to Christ. I will conclude by acknowledging the powerful associations that particular titles have, and suggest that when we apply these to God as metaphors we indicate a crucial difference between the divine and the human.

A CASE STUDY OF THE USE AND EFFECT
OF INCLUSIVE LANGUAGE IN LITURGY

Of the explicit references to God the Holy Trinity in *Worship: from the United Reformed Church*,[2] including prayers with an intentional trinitarian structure, 67 out of 122 references do not name the Father alongside the Son and Holy Spirit but often replace "Father" with "God" or "Creator". In perhaps the most frequently used liturgies—Holy Communion; Service of the Word; Daily Service; and Evening Service—29 out of 41 intentional trinitarian references do not name the Father. A typical example in the Service of the Word from a prayer of adoration is, "God the Creator, we praise you. God in Christ, we turn to you. God the Comforter, we call upon you."[3] And in a blessing we are given the following, ". . . the blessing of the living God, Creator, Redeemer and Spirit be with us all."[4] While another blessing invokes, ". . . the blessing of God, the source of life, of Jesus Christ, the way to life, and of the Holy Spirit, the sustainer of life, is with us today, tomorrow and forever."[5] The intention of these references is to praise and beseech and invoke the blessing of the God who is Trinity. However, in each of these examples the God who is referred to is at risk of being portrayed as less than Trinity. In assigning discrete functions to each person

2. *Worship: from the United Reformed Church* (hereafter cited as *Worship from URC*) is a liturgical resource produced under the auspices of the Doctrine, Prayer and Worship Committee of the United Reformed Church and published in 2003–4. It does not have the status of an official manual (neither did its predecessor *Service Book*, 1989). In its Foreword, John Young states the rationale of the resource: "We now find ourselves in a missionary setting where the church can no longer take for granted that most people understand the religious language and imagery of past generations. Language is changing and the language of worship has to take account of this." If one subscribes to the Protestant principal of the need for worship to be comprehensible and understood, one must commend the intention. What this essay attempts to do is to explore the implications of redescribing God the Holy Trinity using contemporary gender-inclusive language.

3. Ibid., 89.

4. Ibid., 96.

5. Ibid. A former moderator of the General Assembly of the URC was heard to invoke, "the blessing of God, the Maker, the Mender, and the Mover!"

of the Trinity, the works of the Trinity are divided. This contradicts the orthodox trinitarian confession that the works of the Trinity are indivisible. Further, in frequently referring to God in groups of three functions we risk giving the impression that God is modal. Modalism is the heresy[6] that God is an undifferentiated unity and merely acts in different modes. Even when three persons are invoked, it is unorthodox always to assign separate job descriptions to each person of the Trinity. To illustrate this, let us consider the title "Creator." Since the Council of Constantinople in AD 381 agreed what is now commonly known as the Nicene Creed, orthodox Christians have confessed Jesus Christ implicitly as Creator in the phrase, ". . . through him all things were made." Similarly, the confession of the Holy Spirit as consubstantial and coeternal with the Father and Son means that the work of Creation must also be the work of the Spirit. Indeed, "Come, Creator Spirit" is an ancient prayer of the church. Therefore, the term "Creator" as a substitute for "Father" is not equivalent, and, moreover, is functionally misleading if it gives the impression that the first person of the Trinity alone creates. "Source" as an alternative to "Father" has marginally better provenance, since the Son is confessed as eternally begotten of the Father, and the Spirit is confessed as proceeding from the Father. However, even this latter affirmation can be qualified, since the Western church confesses that the Spirit proceeds from the Father *and the Son* (*filioque*). But the main problem with the term "Source" and "Creator" and even "God" as alternatives for "Father" is that they are *impersonal*. Indeed, as we proceed in this discussion, my main criticism of many alternative namings of the trinitarian persons is that in the attempt to be gender inclusive they risk depersonalizing God and as a result risk distancing the worshipper from God. If, as leaders of worship, we distance worshippers from God, we have singularly failed in our calling.

In an essay on the Triune God, Marguerite Shuster makes the following comment that is germane to this discussion, "I reluctantly use male pronouns for God, not because I attribute gender to God or consider God to be more like the male than like the female of the species,

---

6. When I use the term "heresy" I mean a particular belief that an ecumenical council of the church has agreed is an error that risks dividing the church because it undermines the substance of the gospel. In subscribing to this, however, I condemn those actions and attitudes of the "orthodox" toward the "heretics" that are hateful, violent, or unloving, since these constitute a betrayal of the gospel.

but because I worry about the subtle depersonalization that takes place by repeated use of [the terms] 'God' and 'Godself.'"[7] I share Shuster's worry about the issue of depersonalization when functional or neuter terms and pronouns are repeatedly used of God. While it is true that the term "God" is frequently taken by the writers of the New Testament and the creeds to refer to the Father, it is equally true that the term "God" is taken by Christian tradition to refer to the Holy Trinity as a whole. The term "God" is, at best, an equivocal reference to the Father. "God" as a reference to the Father is improved slightly when the adjectives "gracious" or "merciful" are prefixed to it, for these at least tell us of the character of the God to whom we may feel more inclined to draw near. Nevertheless, the terms "Gracious God" and "Merciful God" refer to all three persons in the one being of God and are not distinctive equivalents of the Father. A further pitfall in failing to name the Father in intentionally trinitarian reference is giving the impression that Jesus is fatherless and has no essential relationship to God. In the Second Order of Holy Communion—an order written especially when all ages are present—the first prayer has a threefold structure that is supposed to be trinitarian:

> Loving God,
> you create the world
> and all the people.
> You make bread and wine
> and all good things.
> You are holy and we praise you.
>
> Jesus Christ,
> child of God
> and friend of us all,
> you are with us today
> as we break the bread
> and share the wine
> You are Lord and we love you.
>
> Holy Spirit,
> breath of God,
> moving in all creation,
> you bring us close to God
> and make us holy and strong.
> You are here and we adore you.[8]

7. Shuster, "The Triune God," 1, note 2.

8. *Worship from URC*, 18, © The United Reformed Church, UK, 2003.

The first address is to "Loving God." But we are given no basis upon which the loving God is said to love. One would have thought that a concise New Testament expression could have been adapted here, such as, "Loving God, you love the world so much you sent your only Son."[9] However, the second stanza of the prayer that refers to Jesus Christ re-interprets his relationship to God, preferring to call Jesus "child of God" and not "Son of God." This actually confuses Jesus' identity with that of Christians, since the Christian tradition confesses that Jesus is the incarnation of God's Son by eternal generation;[10] Christians are adopted as God's children by trusting in Christ.[11] The alternative prayer of praise in the same order contains the following phrase, "Loving God, Lord Jesus, Holy Spirit, we worship you, the one holy and eternal God."[12] Here a generic God is affirmed as loving, but there is no essential relation-ship suggested between the Lord Jesus and the loving God. In fact in the whole of this particular liturgy for Holy Communion, God the Father is never once mentioned. While the liturgist has done well in simplifying the language and thereby making this liturgy more accessible to all ages, it is a pity that a likely over-protective attitude to children's imaginations has resulted in the excision of the Father, as well as the neutering and, arguably, the infantilizing of Christ. If any were capable of making an imaginative leap between a human father and God as Father, one would have thought that children were capable. Kathryn Greene-McCreight comments, ". . . most children have more supple imaginations and are therefore better at grasping . . . theological concepts than many adults."[13] It is because of Jesus' witness to God the Father as loving that we confess Jesus as the Son and God as loving. But when this essential relationship

9. My amendment, drawing upon John 3:16.

10. "We believe in one Lord Jesus Christ, the only Son of God, eternally begotten of the Father," The Nicene Creed.

11. "The Spirit you have received is not a spirit of slavery, leading you back into a life of fear, but a Spirit of adoption, enabling us to cry 'Abba! Father!'" Rom 8:15 REB. The Fourth Gospel develops this idea to convey that the new relationship with God made possible through trust in Christ constitutes a new birth "from God" (John 1:13) and therefore a second birth "from above" (John 3:3,7). However, the Fourth Evangelist is careful to distinguish Christians as God's children (*tekna*) from the incarnate Word who is the Father's only-begotten (*monogenous*). It is because the incarnate Word is only-begotten that he gives those who trust in him the power to become children of God (See John 1:12).

12. *Worship from URC*, 19.

13. Greene-McCreight, "What's the story?" 104.

of Son and Father is not referred to, we have no basis on which to say that God is loving, nor that Jesus is the Son of God. This same criticism applies also to the blessing at the conclusion of the same order:

> The blessing of God be upon you,
> the One who loves you,
> the Christ who calls you
> the Spirit who makes you holy,
> today and always.[14]

Here the reference to "God" is intentionally that of the Holy Trinity, but what follows is not a trinitarian but a triadic formula.[15] We must assume that the "One" who loves us is the Father, for we are given nothing more to go on. There is no necessary relationship between the One and Christ, or between the One and Christ and the Spirit. When I say the formula is *triadic* I mean that the structure is deliberately threefold but there is no essential intra-trinitarian relationship between the three being invoked. The risk run by triadic formulations such as this is that since no essential relationship between the three trinitarian persons is established, three gods are being referred to, which is the heresy of tritheism.[16] This same blessing could be significantly improved with a minimum of alteration, such as the following:

> The blessing of God be upon you:
> the motherly Father who loves you
> through Christ, the Son, who calls you
> in the Spirit, who makes you holy,
> today and always.[17]

This altered blessing attempts to invoke the blessing of God the Holy Trinity by an affirmation of the personal operation of the motherly Father (i.e., who is neither male nor female) who loves us *through* the

---

14. *Worship from URC*, 27.

15. I am indebted to Kathryn Greene-McCreight for making a distinction between triadic and trinitarian references to God, see "What's the story?" 103.

16. The author of the cited liturgy has written elsewhere, "I used trinitarian structures and forms, and worked, as I always do, to use ways of writing about God that emphasize the relationality at the heart of God, but without using Father/Son language." Durber, "An Inclusive Communion Order," 43. Here, perhaps, we must agree to disagree. I argue that this particular formulation is triadic, rather than trinitarian, and that there is no essential relationality between the three being invoked.

17. My amendment.

Son, who calls us *in* the Holy Spirit, who makes us holy. It attempts to affirm the fully inter-related and mutually involved nature of all three triune persons. It deliberately stands in the tradition of Athanasius, affirming that the blessing, loving, and calling of God proceeds *from* the Father *through* the Son *in* the Spirit. This economy of the Holy Trinity finds its answer when God enables us to offer our worship and prayer and service *in* the Spirit *through* the Son *to* the Father. A pertinent question to ask of the gender-inclusive references to God we have examined above is this: in what sense can liturgy that has inadvertently or deliberately loosed itself from trinitarian moorings claim to be Christian?

THE FATHER AND PATRIARCHY

The author of the all-age communion liturgy cited above has written elsewhere that one of principles that guided the writing of this liturgy was that of opposing patriarchy. "I did not believe that a liturgy with the express purpose of welcoming children to the table could be framed in words from the 'domination system' of patriarchy . . . the language of patriarchy is not simply pastorally unfortunate for a few abused or sensitive women, but is the language of a dangerous and sinful system in which many human beings are radically oppressed."[18] Similarly, Susan White writes, "For feminist theologians and liturgists, the word *Father* represents a whole history of patriarchal dominance in church and society . . . most of those concerned with the patriarchal associations of the word *Father* have simply advocated the abandonment of *Father* altogether as being 'too hot to handle,' opting for the undifferentiated *God* as the designator for the mystery of the Trinity."[19] While Janet Soskice argues, "Perhaps the most persistent criticism from feminist theologians is that the doctrine of the Trinity is used to reinforce hierarchy and underwrite the maleness of God."[20] And Jane Williams adds, ". . . thoughtless and careless use of male imagery about God has an actively oppressive effect, and leaves many people feeling that they cannot love or be loved by such a God. Male imagery in general may have this effect, particularly

18. Durber, "An Inclusive Communion Order," 43.

19. White, *Whatever happened to the Father?*, 13–14. After stating the feminist case for inclusive references to God, White goes on to offer a critique of worship that omits all references to God the Father as neglecting the essential trinitarian dynamic of Christian worship.

20. Soskice, "Trinity and Feminism," 138.

on women, who feel themselves excluded from the task of imaging God in the world; fatherhood language is particularly exacerbated example of this, bringing with it, to all kinds of people, the damaging experience of human parenting."[21] If the proclamation of the gospel—a gospel that is supposed to liberate—evokes a sense of oppression and exclusion and alienation due to changes in the language in which it is couched; then translation and reinterpretation is urgently required.[22] If we accept this premise, however, then not only the gospel but also much of the Christian tradition based on it also requires translation and reinterpretation. For example, how would feminists regard the following argument from Calvin? "True godliness . . . consists . . . of a pure and true zeal which loves God as a real Father and looks up to him as a real Lord; it embraces his righteousness and detests offending him more than it does dying. And all those who have this zeal do not set about rashly fabricating a god in line with their own wishes. Instead they have knowledge of the true God from God himself, and do not conceive of him as being different from what he reveals himself to be and what he makes known to them."[23] The temptation to "fabricate a god in line with one's own wishes" is a perennial one; but are feminists any more at risk of yielding to it than anyone else? Calvin's argument is partly a warning against allowing false notions of God to interpose themselves in our thinking (which would be a form of idolatry); partly a call to be faithful to the nature of God revealed to us in the Scriptures. Put colloquially, "It's not a matter of the God you want; it's a matter of the God you've got." Both the critics and detractors of Christianity, when they care to look, can find biblical material suggesting that God is hierarchical, dominating, and excluding. However, the way Christian doctrine develops—especially the doctrine of the Trinity—reinterprets and builds on biblical material to advocate an understanding of the Father, Son, and Spirit as equal, loving, and inclusive.

21. Williams, "The Fatherhood of God," 166.

22. Contrast this with the experience of Bilquis Sheikh, who writes of her conversion from what she perceived as the patriarchy of Islam to the liberation of the loving Father of Jesus Christ. See Sheikh, *I Dared to Call Him Father*.

23. Calvin, *Brève Instruction chrétienne*, 4–5.

THE DOCTRINE OF THE TRINITY
AS THE SUBVERSION OF PATRIARCHY

Janet Soskice argues that a proper understanding of God as Trinity can serve to guard against the stifling androcentrism and the gross anthropocentrism that mistakes the divine persons as male officers in a hierarchy. Soskice claims that the trinitarian baptismal formula ". . . the name of the Father and of the Son and of the Holy Spirit"[24] contains the seeds of its own self-subversion. We are baptized "in the name" (singular), not in the names (plural) of two men and a mysterious third.[25] The understanding of the being of the Holy Trinity as *perichoresis* (*circumincessio*) is the antithesis of hierarchical exercises of power. Father, Son, and Holy Spirit do not attempt to dominate one another and others; rather, they give to and receive from one another their personhood as an eternal expression of self-giving love. The Father generates the Son and sends the Holy Spirit. The Son is eternally begotten of the Father and becomes incarnate of the Holy Spirit. The Holy Spirit proceeds from the Father and the Son, and completes the work of the Father through the Son.[26] The personhood of each divine person is what it is only in relation to the other two. Some have claimed that this self-giving mutuality is an inherent critique of patriarchy. Whether one agrees with this claim or not, the contrast between this understanding of God and the understanding of the distant monad-god of deism could hardly be greater. We would all fear an aloof judge who cares not a whit about our welfare but threatens to destroy us in his anger. This is not the God Paul presents to us in Romans 8. Paul presents God as one who does not condemn those united to Christ. God accepts these into his family by the indwelling Spirit of adoption as full co-heirs with Christ. The Spirit's action within these causes them both to cry out to God as "Abba" and interprets to God their inarticulate groans. This is the God who is "on our side" and "who acquits" and whose

24. Matt 28:19b.

25. Soskice, Ibid., 139.

26. In the being of God the Holy Trinity, as the Christian tradition understands it, there is no sense that the Father dominates the Son and the Spirit, but there is a sense of *order*. This order—from the Father through the Son in the Spirit—does not impair the freedom of the divine persons. Rather, loving order is the mode through which the the freedom of God is exercised. This has obvious implications for the life of the church, as the report of the Report of the Anglican-Reformed International Commission 1984 puts it, ". . . order is love in regulative operation, and love is the fundamental reality of the church's being." *God's Reign and Our Unity*, 52 §82.

judgment is expressed in Christ dying and being raised from death for us.[27] When Paul's incipient trinitarian theology is placed alongside the Johannine theology of mutual indwelling (the Spirit of Truth in believers, Christ in the Father, believers in Christ, Christ in believers[28]); and the Johannine emphasis on love ("God is love; those who dwell in love dwell in God and God in them.")[29] one can see why the trinitarian theology of *perichoresis* developed as it did. The dominant note that sounds in both the biblical sources used and in trinitarian doctrine as it develops is *personal love*. The conundrum we face is that, for some, the language of "Father, Son, and Holy Spirit" does not evoke personal love but evokes something rather different.

GENDER AND GENDER-BENDING

Our language is gendered because it arises from our human experience in which masculinity and femininity, along with male and female sexual distinction, are fundamental to our human identity.[30] It is in this sense that we are personal. Most of us are raised in families in which mothers and fathers, sisters and brothers, deeply shape our character. However, God, being uncreated and incorporeal spirit, is not constrained by a material body and is not personal in the same way that humans are. The Christian tradition teaches that God is personal as the Trinity of Father, Son, and Holy Spirit: a perichoretic communion of three spiritual persons in one being. Yet the language we deploy to refer to the Holy Trinity is human language shaped by the complementary binaries of female and male, feminine and masculine, mother and father, sister and brother, and daughter and son. God has created the sexual distinctions that characterize the created world; however, God, in God's own being, is not

27. See Rom 8:14–33 NRSV.

28. See John 14:15–26.

29. 1 John 4:16b, my translation.

30. I take for granted the binaries of male/female sexual distinction, including transsexual or hermaphrodite, as being principally a matter of physiology (which does not exclude the psychological). Gender, on the other hand, is increasingly recognized as being far more plastic than sexual distinction, being largely a matter of the social convention attached to being female or male. I favor regarding gender as a continuum between femininity and masculinity, with each of us locating ourselves on a different point of this continuum, including the transgendered. And yet, for the Christian, it cannot be emphasized too strongly that these distinctions of sex and gender are secondary to our primary identity "in Christ."

constrained by these sexual distinctions. While God is not constrained by created sexual distinctions, there is nonetheless the striking implication in the first chapter of Genesis that male and female human beings together constitute the image of God.[31] In the context of our discussion, this would suggest that the complementary female-male human relationship reflects God's image in the created sphere. Christian theologians have drawn a parallel between this fundamental human relationship and the relationship believed to constitute the Holy Trinity: both share a creative complementarity of persons. When they are considered together, the many and varied references to God in the Scriptures constitute a belief in God that is much broader than a singular male-like identity. This should be taken into account when we consider the New Testament writers' frequent use of terms "Father" and "Son" when referring to God and Christ. Against the background of the strong tradition in the Scriptures prohibiting idolatry, we should not assume that it is legitimate to use human fatherhood to circumscribe God's Fatherhood or human sonship to circumscribe Christ's Sonship. That is to say, we should not assume that our experience of human fatherhood and sonship are circles into which we can neatly place God's Fatherhood or Christ's Sonship. The biblical writers, and Christ himself, one assumes, used the terms father and son because these were terms readily understandable to communicate the intimate and essential relationship that Jesus claimed to have with God. But in the Gospels there is recognition that God is "Father" in a unique sense. Matthew ascribes to Jesus the prohibition, "Do not call any man on earth 'father', for you have one Father, and he is in heaven."[32] This should make us pause when considering the relationship between human fathers and God as heavenly Father. It suggests that taking human fatherhood as the template for God's Fatherhood is the wrong way round. Rather than saying that God is like a human father, we should say that a good father or mother is like God.[33] God is ". . . the Father, from whom every family in heaven and on earth derives its name."[34] Human fathers and mothers aspire to the consistent loving-kindness,

31. "God created human beings in his own image; in the image of God he created them; male and female he created them." Gen 1:27 REB.

32. Matt 23:9 REB.

33. I am indebted to the Reverend Robert Courtney for this point.

34. Ephesians 3:14–15, my translation. There is word-play in the Greek on Father (*Patera*) and family (*patria*).

grace, and justice of God. Understood this way, the faults and failings of human fathers need not rule out the term "Father" when used of God. According to the Apostle Paul, central to our spiritual/logical worship is the offering of the self to God and the determination not to be conformed to the patterns of one's era but to be transformed by the renewal of one's mind.[35] Worship is the act in which we corporately receive the Father's Word in the Spirit, and respond in that same Spirit to the Word by corporately offering the self in faith and penitence to the Father. The cumulative effect of such worship is that we—including our thinking and concepts—begin to be transformed. In worship we come to realize that God the Father is the original and unique Type; this name can be applied to human fathers only analogically. Or, arguing from the other end, "Father" should be used of God apophatically, ". . . by means of a determined 'thinking away' of the inappropriate—and in this context, that means masculine—connotations of the term."[36] As one of my theological teachers used to say, "There is no maleness in God the Father."[37]

Substituting "Mother" instead of "Father", as some have done, while having the merit of being personal, arguably risks exchanging patriarchy for matriarchy. Instead of the misconceived attempt to import human power-relations into the Godhead, we would do better to reflect on Christ's command "Be perfect as your heavenly Father is perfect."[38] This command challenges us to let our heavenly Father's character, as revealed through Christ in the Spirit—a character of service and sacrificial love—to reshape and reform our human notions and practices of fatherhood, motherhood, sonship, and daughterhood. Jürgen Moltmann argues that there are two different bases for the use of the name "Father" for God: the first is a patriarchal world-view; the second is a trinitarian understanding through Christ.[39] If God as "Father" is understood as being at the apex of a pyramid that legitimates the patriarchal rights and power of males in church, state, and family, one can understand why feminists and others would reject God as Father. By contrast, Moltmann argues that the Christian understanding of God as Father is based on a

35. See Romans 12:1–2

36. "The Report of the British Council of Churches Study Commission on Trinitarian Doctrine Today," 37.

37. Professor Alan Torrance.

38. Matt 5:48, my translation.

39. Moltmann, *History and the Triune God*, 19.

trinitarian understanding of God through the person of Jesus Christ.[40]
Moltmann also points out that in the Christian dogmatic tradition God
the Father has occasionally been attributed with an idiomatically ma-
ternal function in relation to the Son. The Council of Toledo in AD 675
confessed, "We must believe that the Son was not made out of nothing,
nor out of some substance or other, but from the womb of the Father,
that is, that he was begotten or born from the Father's own being." The
theologians at Toledo were, presumably, not ignorant of human anatomy
but were attempting to make an important theological statement about
the identity of being that the Son shares with the Father. In so doing
they incidentally reveal an understanding of God the Father that both
encompasses and transcends human male/female sexual categories.
Moltmann comments that such an understanding would suggest that
God the Father is bisexual or transsexual.[41] These terms, however, run
the risk of being misunderstood and commandeered in order to advance
particular political ends. Paul Molnar warns about the risk of using God
as a symbol that we recreate in order to achieve a desired social, political,
or religious end. He argues that the attempt to commandeer God in the
service of one's own agenda is sinful insofar as it opposes the action of
God to create new hearts within us according to God's purposes and
goals.[42] Rather than attempting to use God to legitimate our particular purpose or perspective or identity, it would be far better to think of
God as meta-sexual and meta-gendered. That is to say, while we can,
and must, use terms from human experience to refer to God; God, as
Creator, is above, and therefore not constrained by, created sexual distinction and human configurations of gender.

FAMILY AND ALLEGIANCE

Having said all this, and writing as a pastor, I also recognize that theological argument is not necessarily the most effective way of approach-
ing worshippers for whom the term "Father" constitutes a barrier when
referring to God, some who testify to dysfunctional and abusive relationship with their father, others who wish to express solidarity with
those who suffer as a result of patriarchal domination. However, I have

40. See Moltmann, Ibid., 20–2.

41. See Moltmann, Ibid., 22.

42. See Molnar, *Divine Freedom and the Doctrine of the Immanent Trinity*, 18–9.

also encountered those who have had dysfunctional and abusive relationships with their mother (and in some cases a brother or sister also),
for whom the term "Mother" when applied to God is just as problematic.
Terms such as father, mother, brother, and sister will have strong associations, since these relationships and these persons significantly shape
our character for better or for worse. How can we adopt a sensitive pastoral approach to such persons while at the same time leading them into
the presence of a God whom they can worship? One possible response
is to suggest that part of the liberating power of the gospel is found in
responding to its call to form a new allegiance. This new allegiance is
formed by trusting in Christ and takes priority over allegiances to family, and therefore also takes priority over the demands of patriarchy and
matriarchy. Still today, Jesus' challenge to his would-be disciples sounds
harsh, "No one is worthy of me who cares more for father or mother than
for me; no one is worthy of me who cares more for son or daughter."[43]
At the time, Jesus' challenge was both scandalous and revolutionary. To
Jews, the honoring of one's parents was commanded by God;[44] while the
striking or cursing of one's parents were capital offences.[45] For Romans,
the *Paterfamilias* exercised absolute power over his family. In Jesus'
challenge to his would-be followers to make their relationship with him
pre-eminent, he was simultaneously calling them to *reprioritize* biological family ties, including challenging the expectation that one should
automatically obey the demands of a patriarch or matriarch. In our own
time, when the church is automatically assumed to be "pro-family", we
have perhaps not yet fully realized the implications of Jesus' challenge.
Jesus is not advocating the neglect of one's family; he is indicating that
allegiance to him requires a radical reconfiguration of all our loyalties.
Whereas we were once at the beck-and-call of our families and had no
choice but to obey their demands (or, perhaps our family had no choice
but to obey our demands); now our first allegiance is to Christ, whose
"yoke is easy" and whose "burden is light." Moreover, Christ superim-
poses new spiritual ties over our biological ties. Through Christ we are
adopted into the church, the family of God, and with Christ we find that,
"Whoever does the will of God is my brother and sister and mother."[46]

43. Matt 10:37 REB.

44. See Exod 20:12.

45. See Exod 21:15, 17.

46. Mark 3:35 REB.

Perhaps most challenging of all is when Jesus extends the command to love, encompassing not only family and friends but also enemies, ". . . Love your enemies; do good to those who hate you; bless those who curse you; pray for those who treat you spitefully."[47] Those obligations previously regarded as owed only to one's nearest and dearest are now owed also to those who revile and oppress us. Strikingly, in the command to love, to do good, to bless, and to pray for one's persecutors, we have the seeds of the overturning of all oppressive power-relations. Those who oppress and bully operate on the assumption that those under their power will think and behave in certain ways: that of cowed compliance. Jesus calls for a revolutionary change in attitude and action toward those who oppress us: we are not to hate them, nor cower before them, but love them. The implication of this new way of treating those who oppose is profoundly political. Instead of interactions characterized by fear, resentment, rivalry, and partisanship; we are called to love, forgive, cooperate, and be genuinely open to the other.

ASSOCIATIONS AND METAPHOR

However, again, writing as a pastor, I know that it is one thing to love and forgive those who have hurt us; it is quite another to loosen the hold that *associations* may have upon us. One may accept that the title "Father" is used of God in way that is different to the way one uses it of one's natural father, yet be unable fully to free one's imagination from the powerful association that the title has. Indeed, as Jane Williams argues, "One of the great drawbacks of narrative, pictorial language is that you cannot regulate the picture your hearer makes."[48] As preachers can testify, to their cost: a supposedly innocuous illustration can conjure an unintended meaning due to a peculiar association it has for a hearer. Consider the parallel of choosing a name for a newborn baby daughter or son. Parents will often rule out particular names because of the association that those names have with people they dislike or for other reasons. Similarly, it would be naïve to believe that one could expunge every trace of association that the title "father" conjures in one's imagination. And yet, part of the power of metaphor is the imaginative leap required to apply the qualities of one thing to another. There are many ways in

---

47. Luke 6:27–8 REB.
48. Williams, Ibid., 172.

which God is obviously unlike the human male progenitor of children; yet there are also many ways in which God is like the human father who gives life, loves, and provides for his children. The key, I believe, is the *recognition of the gap* between the two subjects of the metaphor. In the case of a human father and God our heavenly Father, the gap is infinite. There is no route from the spatio-temporal to the eternal. Indeed, God would be completely unknowable and unreachable had not God bridged the gap and made himself present in space-time through the incarnation of his Word and present to space-time by the action of his Holy Spirit. It is thus on the basis of God's self-revelation to humanity, necessarily involving the commandeering of human language, that we may know God and speak of God. God's revelation is always filtered through the prisms of culture, time, and place. If we are to understand aright what God wishes to reveal to us in our culture, time, and place, then we will need to use language and concepts that are fit for purpose. As we engage in this demanding and on-going task, we need the self-critical and prophetic courage to name the particular power-relations, abuses, inequalities, prejudices, and assumptions that exert their power in our culture and era. In its twentieth-century form, feminism was a reaction against assumed masculine prerogatives of power and normalcy. This has been a needed and helpful reaction and corrective. The Scriptures were written in epochs and cultures with particular assumptions. Biblical scholars, social historians, feminists, and others help us to identify where these assumptions differ from our own assumptions.

While operating within the linguistic and cultural conventions of their times, the biblical writers yet testify to new realities—the Incarnation; the kingdom of God; the gospel; the life of the age to come—that both critique and explode their linguistic and cultural conventions. The fact that many today would not find the following statement arresting and surprising—"there is no longer Jew or Greek, there is no longer slave or free, there is no longer male and female; for all of you are one in Christ Jesus"[49]—reveals just how much of our thinking and culture has been shaped by it. At the time Paul was writing, what many found so shocking and offensive is the suggestion that Gentiles, slaves, and women are, by faith in Christ, given full status as sons (and thus as heirs, since only *sons* were eligible to inherit) of God their heavenly Father. This is precisely what some contemporary Christian feminists find shocking and

49. Gal 3:28 NRSV.

offensive, but for different reasons! They argue that they are not sons but daughters and that the term Father used of God is so tainted by patriarchy that it excludes and alienates them. This brings us back to our dilemma. On the one hand, when Jesus and the writers of the New Testament used term "Father" of God, they did so in order to herald a new relationship of intimacy that Jesus had with God, a relationship in which all are invited to share through trust in Jesus *without exclusion.* On the other hand, today we find that this same relationship with God the Father in which we invite people to share through trust in Jesus, along with the pronoun "he" used of God, is at risk of *excluding* some current and would-be followers of Jesus for whom the title "Father" is alienating. How should we respond to this dilemma? I have already suggested the responses of deploying the doctrine of the Trinity to subvert patriarchy; of realizing the liberating effect of allegiance to Christ; and of noting that when we use the metaphor of Father there is an infinite difference between the divine and the human. Another response is to emphasize the importance of *continuity* in the Christian tradition.

> [The Christian] conception of God is centered upon the "Father" of Jesus. While it is perfectly acceptable for Christians to apply to God feminine images, characteristic of motherhood, and to use the pronoun "she" at times, including in prayer, since all our language is metaphorical or analogical, it remains true that privileging the idea of divine fatherhood, and other related gendered language, derives from the main root of specifically Christian theism. Its eradication would threaten linguistic and spiritual continuity with Jesus, unappealing as this conclusion may be to some forms of feminist theology.[50]

If we claim to be Christian we are implicitly claiming continuity with the person and teaching of Jesus, central to which is the new relationship with God the Father that Jesus heralded. The revolutionary message of the Christian gospel is that through trust in Christ we are adopted by God as daughters and sons, each being given the same status as Jesus.[51] Having been made right with God through Christ, there are no second-class or third-class or fourth-class citizens. Through faith in Christ, all Christians have equal access in prayer to "Our Father in heaven." However, one could maintain continuity with the Christian tradition

---

50. Hastings, "God," 273.
51. See Rom 8:14–7, 29.

whilst also innovating in order to take account of contemporary objections. For example, one could refer to God as our "motherly Father."[52] This would signal, by way of analogy,[53] the belief that God has both motherly and fatherly qualities but is no more female than male.

CONCLUSION

The church runs a considerable risk when it adjusts its doctrine of God in liturgy in the effort to avoid the taint of patriarchy. There are more effective ways that the church can address the issue of patriarchy: one-to-one listening and discussion; on-going love of those who hold an understanding that is different than one's own understanding; and structural/political action to challenge all forms of oppression. Liturgy is at its least pastoral and political, and is least effective as a vehicle for worship, when it gives the impression that God is an impersonal triad of three functionaries or a modalist monad of three functions. Liturgy is at its most pastoral and political when it presents as clearly as it can the character of God the Holy Trinity. The trinitarian God is the communion of three persons in one being. Father, Son, and Holy Spirit continually give to and receive from one another their personhood in a manner completely unlike the exercise of human hierarchy and patriarchy. The nature of the Holy Trinity, therefore, serves both as critique and subversion of hierarchy and patriarchy when, through trust in Christ, we share in the Trinity's self-giving love and in so doing spurn the way of domination. This forms part of our response to the call of the gospel, requiring a new allegiance to Christ that, in turn, challenges us to reconfigure all our relationships. "Father" is a term that derives from one of our most formative human relationships. As such, it will have strong resonances and associations. However, God the Father is the original and unique Type; the same name should be used of human fathers only by way of analogy, acknowledging that there is an infinite difference between the divine and the human. The difference or gap between categorically dif-

---

52. This is Moltmann's solution in *History and the Triune God*, 22.

53. Following the lead of Thomas Aquinas, one may argue that the terms that the biblical writers apply to God such as lion, shepherd, rock, and fortress are analogies that draw meaning and power from their strong associations in human experience. God manifests strength in his works, as a lion in his; God cares and guides as a shepherd does; God is as steadfast as a rock; God is a fortress in which we take refuge. This analogical approach may also be helpful when we use gendered human language of God. See Aquinas, *Summa Theologica*, 1a, 13.

ferent beings is where metaphor can be usefully employed. In metaphor a deliberate imaginative leap is required to apply the qualities of one thing to another. A modest proposal in the attempt to overcome the apparent impasse between feminists and traditionalists is the use of title "motherly Father". This tries to take into account feminist objections whilst also striking a note of continuity with New Testament usage and Christian tradition. Making more use of the address "Heavenly Father" could emphasize that God's Fatherhood is of a different order than human fatherhood.[54] I recognize that these suggestions may be going too far for some; while for others, they will not be going far enough. We may never agree about this, yet I dare to hope and pray that we can respect one another's different points-of-view in Christian love, maintaining fellowship with one another in Christ.[55] The doctrine of the Trinity teaches us that unity need not enforce homogeneity; rather, personal distinctiveness may enrich unity.

54. Pronouns used of God are more problematic. The neuter pronoun "it" has the considerable drawback of both objectifying and depersonalizing the persons of whom it is used, and is therefore not an attractive option. Using "she" and "her" as pronouns for God may be shocking for some, and therefore runs the risk of alienating a proportion of the Christian constituency—the feminist conundrum in reverse. Using "he" and "his" as pronouns for God stands in continuity with the biblical and Christian tradition, and may be preferred, if only because it is the least problematic option.

55. This essay is the expanded and revised version of a short paper presented to the 2007 conference 'Reforming Worship'. The short paper provoked a discussion with the author of the "Second Order for Holy Communion," one of the objects of my theological critique. An ecumenical respondent later reflected on the exchange between the author and myself, commenting that we had "disagreed well," showing respect for one another; an attitude not always evident in debates between Christians.

5

Who Does What? Presidency
at the Sacraments in the Reformed Tradition[1]

Recent Changes in the United Reformed Church

BY KEITH RIGLIN

ALTHOUGH THE TWO PRINCIPAL traditions which came together in
the United Reformed Church in 1972 have different origins, they
held closely to the concept that ordination was to the one ministry
of Word and sacrament within the church catholic, a position which
is still maintained by the United Reformed Church, in common with
other churches of the Reformed tradition. In this essay I discuss the process that eventually led the General Assembly of the United Reformed
Church of 1998 to amend its *Basis of Union*, following a resolution at
the previous Assembly to which no objection by synods had been regis-
tered, to include the following statement concerning "Presidency at the
Sacraments in an Emergency":

> The provisions of paragraph 24 [in the Basis of Union] are in-
> tended to establish the principle that worship should be led by
> representative persons recognized by the wider church as well as
> by the local church. The provisions do not prevent the congre-
> gation assembled for a baptismal or Communion service from
> themselves appointing, as a church meeting, a suitable person
> to preside at the celebration of the sacrament in a case of emer-

1. The subject of this essay was a matter of lively debate at the *Reforming Worship*
conference. The original paper presented, "The Saints' Everlasting Rest: The Reformed
Position," may be found in McLaughlin and Pinnock, *Mary and Ecumenism*, 62–74.

gency, for example if the expected president is taken ill or held up in travel. The provisions do not require such an action rather than a postponement of the baptismal or Communion service if that seems preferable.[2]

It will be argued that this resolution, and the thoughts and practices behind it, display a practice of authority and order in a Reformed church different from the inherited traditions of both Congregationalism and Presbyterianism. Although this essay does address the issue of "lay presidency"—a matter of disagreement between the two churches which formed the United Reformed Church in 1972—its primary interest is to see how this new position of 1998 connects with traditional Reformed understandings of the character of the ordained ministry in the antecedent traditions, the peculiar role of district councils—as "presbyteries"—and the apparent revival of the authoritative status of the church meeting. As a member of the General Assembly at the time of the change, and as the minister of a charge in which the matter was both discussed and challenged, reference is made to events leading up to the change. Who does what in church is a matter affecting all churches, not least the Reformed, and the decisions and practice of the United Reformed Church will surely contribute to the discussions within those other churches.

ORDINATION AND THE MINISTRY

For Presbyterians, ordination was a rite properly presided over by "presbyters orderly associated;"[3] an act of the presbytery. For Congregationalists, whose concept of the local church moved not beyond the locally gathered congregation—alone to be spoken of as "church"—ordination to the ministry was celebrated in the local church and by the local church. It was also seen, at least for some within this tradition, as not so much an act conferring grace as recognition of grace already received. For example, addressing the Assembly of the Congregational Union in 1921 the then chairman remarked, "Ordination . . . is not a rite that makes a ministry valid and confers authority. It is rather a rite which recognizes an authority resident in the [local] church and delegated by it to one

---

2. Resolution 10, URC, *Record* (1998).

3. *Form of Presbyteral Church-Government of 1647.* Thompson, *Stating the Gospel,* 12–60.

who is to act with the church and for it."[4] Thus, in any discussion on the principles concerning presidency (including "lay presidency") at the sacraments, this understanding of the origins of the ministry and ordination—indeed, of any authorized ministry within the church—is important to note. If, for example, the minister, as the local pastor, is simply exercising an authority which is "resident in the [local] church and delegated by it" to him or her, then a situation where the same local church, through its church meeting,[5] authorizes someone other than the ordained minister to preside at celebrations of the sacrament seems at most a departure from the regular pattern. However, for those who believe that the ministry of Word and sacrament—be it that of ordained ministers and pastors in Reformed churches or that of bishops and presbyters in episcopally ordered churches such as those of the Anglican Communion—begins essentially with a commission from Christ exercised through the conferring of grace in a rite of ordination, "lay" presidency is far more problematic.

Whereas it would be untrue to suggest that this second view is, or has ever been, the only or even the dominant view amongst Presbyterians, it is certainly the case that ordination to the ministry by prayer and the laying on of hands of already ordained presbyters—"presbyters orderly associated"[6]—has been regarded as an essential mark of a church claiming a Presbyterian polity. Amongst Congregationalists this has not always been the case. For example, the propositions of the first conference of the Faith and Order Movement of 1927 included the statement:

> The ministry is a gift of God through Christ to his church and is essential to the being and well-being of the church . . . Men [sic] gifted for the work of ministry, called by the Spirit and accepted by the church, are commissioned through an act of ordination by prayer and the laying on of hands.

To this the Congregational Union of England and Wales responded:

4. A. J. Viner, Chairman of the Congregational Union of England and Wales in 1921. Tucker, *Reformed Ministry*, 31.

5. For Congregationalists, the "church meeting" is the place where the authority of Christ is expressed in the only body which can legitimately be spoken of as "church." See Dale, *A Manual of Congregational Disciplines*, 11.

6. Concerning the Doctrinal Part of Ordination of Ministers, *The Form of Presbyteral Church Government* (1684) §10.

> We hold that to the church as a society of believers no special ministry is strictly essential . . . Ordination [and] the accompanying practice of the laying on of hands, though quite usual among us, is not regarded as obligatory.[7]

The contrast with the former Presbyterian Church of England is striking.

> Christ hath instituted a government, and governors ecclesiastical in the church . . . It is lawful, and agreeable to the Word of God . . . The scripture doth hold out a presbytery in a church.[8]

Such a difference in the need, or otherwise, for ordination by the laying on of hands is seen in the terms of the Covenant of 1951 between the Congregationalists and Presbyterians of England. Under the section dealing with ministerial eligibility, whereas it is simply stated, "A minister in good standing of the Presbyterian Church of England . . . is eligible for a call from a member church of the Congregational Union," further conditions are laid for the reverse. "A minister on the roll of ministers of the Congregational Union of England and Wales *who has been baptized and ordained* . . . is eligible for a call to a charge in the Presbyterian Church."[9] The Presbyterians were clear that, for them at least, ordination was essential for the recognition and authorization of a minister;

---

7. Congregational Union, *Year Book*. A different understanding, also from the Congregationalist tradition, is given by the Baptist ecclesiologist Neville Clark. "Of 'ministries' there may and will be many; but the ordained ministry constitutes a special and constant gift of the ascended Lord to his church . . . Theologically the minister is not essentially a congregational figure. He is the representative of the one body set within the congregation to promote its christological ordering and edification in love, and as such he is the living embodiment of catholicity. Ordained by the whole church for the service of the whole church, he brings to a focus within the life of the congregation the *episcope* of her Lord." *The Pattern of the Church*, 99, 107. Baptist liturgy has been strongly influenced by the Reformed tradition, seen in *Orders and Prayers for Church Worship: A Manual for Ministers* published in 1960, which draws heavily upon Reformed liturgies, notably the 1940 edition of the *Book of Common Order* of the Church of Scotland. The title (and contents) of later Baptist liturgical sources—*Patterns and Prayers for Christian Worship: A Guidebook for Worship Leaders*, 1980, and *Gathering for Worship: Patterns and Prayer for the Community of Disciples*, 2005—demonstrate the move away from the language (and form) of Reformed liturgy.

8. *The Form of Presbyteral Church Government*, approved by the General Assembly of the Church of Scotland in 1645. Together with *The Directory for the Publick Worship of God* approved the same year and *The Confession of Faith* (The "Westminster Confession") approved in 1647, it forms the basis of Presbyterian faith and order. Thompson, op. cit.

9. Presbyterian Church of England, *The Book of Order*, 8. The italics are mine.

for Congregationalists (at least in the 1950s and 60s), it is similarly clear this was not the case.

> This church [the Presbyterian Church of England] has always faithfully maintained and practiced the rite of ordination to the holy ministry as an act of presbytery to be accompanied by the laying on of hands according to ancient and scriptural use; and this order of ordination this church (without thereby condemning other churches which do not observe it) does not propose to relinquish, but on the contrary adheres to it, as a form right and scriptural in itself, and also as an element contributing to a basis of common order among different sections of the church.[10]

Prior to the 1972 formation of the United Reformed Church it was therefore possible for persons to be listed on the Congregational Union's roll of ministers without having been ordained; a situation which could not have arisen amongst Presbyterians. For those Congregationalist ministers who were ordained (by far the majority) it was the practice for ordination to be celebrated when inducted to their first charges, presided over by a minister from another local church, assisted in the act of ordination by other ministers present, and sometimes by members of the local diaconate.[11] However, such different emphases in understanding the authority in ordination account, in part, for the different and differing practices surrounding presidency at the sacrament in the two traditions.[12]

---

10. Ibid., 9.

11. In Congregational (and Baptist) churches deacons exercise a local ministry, elected by the church meeting and commissioned in public worship to serve for the period of their election. There was an early tradition of such deacons being ordained, but the specifically local aspect of the office accounts, in part, for this practice having ceased by the time of the 1972 union. Serving Congregationalist deacons were deemed to be "elders" after the union and offered ordination as such. After their term of service, if not previously ordained as elders, such persons were ordained.

12. In my own experience I have noted how the 1974 *Ministerial Recognition Rules* of the Baptist Union of Great Britain, under which I began my ministry, contained the rule, "When a probationer first settles in a Baptist church there should be a service of ordination"—as there was, when I was ordained in 1983. However, I also note that in the 1991 revision of the *Rules* the reference to ordination has been removed. This removal is entirely consisted with Congregationalism, where ordination, if practiced, whilst celebrated with other local churches and with other ministers representing wider associations or unions of churches, is not essential to the exercise of effective pastoral ministry.

THE POSITION OF THE CHURCHES PRIOR TO UNION

Before the union of 1972 the differing understandings of the essential character of the ordained ministry led to presidency at the sacraments being exercised differently in the two churches. The Presbyterian Church of England, following the almost universal tradition of Reformed churches and the wider church catholic, restricted presidency to those ordained as presbyters, ministers of the Word and sacraments. Such a tradition remains the case in the Church of Scotland,[13] related to the good ordering of the church in which, although the minister presides, the entire community celebrates.[14] In this regard it should be noted that the United Reformed Church—like the Church of Scotland, but unlike the Church of England and the Church of Rome—does not draw a distinction, in matters of presidency, between baptism and the Eucharist.[15]

It was a not dissimilar understanding of good ordering that allowed Congregational churches to adopt a radically different practice. True to one understanding of Congregationalist polity, they believed they could, and some did, set apart whomever the church meeting, or sometimes the diaconate of the local church, invited so to preside. Such a tradition, at least in practice, is relatively new in Congregationalism, emerging amongst English Nonconformity during the nineteenth century. Indeed, it is interesting to note how many so-called traditional marks of Nonconformist celebrations of the Eucharist in Congregationalist churches have their origin at this time—together with lay presidency, monthly celebrations rather than the weekly of earlier centuries, individual communion glasses rather than a common chalice, and unfermented grape juice rather than wine.[16]

13. Act iv, General Assembly of the Church of Scotland (1975). See Herron, *The Law and Practice of the Kirk*, 153–4.

14. As Forsyth comments, when contrasting the Levitical priesthood with Protestant sacraments, "The essential thing is the communal act, the act of communal obedience, in which the priest is the organ of a community priestly without him, and he is but the channel of God." *The Cruciality of the Cross*, 91.

15. Clark, as well as drawing no distinction between baptism and the Eucharist, does not divide the two functions of the ordained presbyter. "Only the ordained minister, called, trained, tested, and commissioned, may rightly preach the liturgical sermon and dispense the dominical sacraments." Clark, op. cit., 109.

16. The origins of these may be in a general reaction against the perceived "catholic" traditions of the Oxford Movement in the Church of England, alongside the development of a peculiar Protestant individualistic piety. Note David Thompson's observation of how some of the early Congregationalist churches would meet for several years with-

Such a practice on presidency is consistent with the Congregation-alist ideal that authority in all things, resides, under God, in the church meeting.

> In Congregational churches, as a matter of priority and order, the pastor always presides at the Lord's Supper; but there is nothing in the New Testament to prevent a church from celebrating the sacrament in the absence of its pastor. An "ordained minister" is not necessary to give validity to the service. The words of Paul (1 Corinthians 10:16) seem to imply that the "blessing" of the cup, though one voice alone may be heard, is the act of the whole church; and that those who break the bread break it as the repre-sentatives of the church.[17]

In 1972 these two traditions were brought together. Given the covenant character of that union and its newness at the time, it seems highly unlikely that such a provision as that agreed in 1998 would have received the assent of the General Assembly in the 1970s or early 1980s. The United Reformed Church was still, at that time, defining itself as Congregational-Presbyterian, was still seeking to develop a common pattern, and was still extremely sensitive to the earlier traditions of the two constituent communions.[18]

By 1998, as in other cases, the self-understanding of the national church as a Reformed church drawing on the richness of both tradi-tions—both ways of being Reformed, as it were—had created a climate where diversity was not only accepted but also affirmed. Thus, whereas some congregations would still not countenance lay presidency, and would therefore see no need for the provision of Resolution 10 of 1998 for itself, they also would not stand in the way of the exercise of such pro-visions by those who convictions were otherwise. They would, however, be concerned to ensure that traditions long cherished were respected.

---

out ever celebrating baptism or the Eucharist because they believed that "sacraments could not be administered until pastors or teachers were ordained in their office." Page 100.

17. Dale, op. cit., 154.

18. The Reformed tradition, in its national church form, has moved on since John Knox's *First Book of Discipline*, 1560, in which was so strong the insistence on the neces-sity for lawful succession in the ministry (i.e., ordination), that those who tampered with "Christ's seals" (i.e., the sacraments) without this duly transmitted commission and authority were "even worthy of death"! Warr, *The Presbyterian Tradition*, 292.

PRESIDENCY AT THE EUCHARIST

The two different understandings of the authority expressed in ordination—that of the local church as an expression of the church catholic, and that of the "presbytery"—were brought together in the conciliar understanding of authority in the United Reformed Church. However, this conciliar model does affect the church's understanding of the nature of the presidency of the ordained minister, especially when compared with that of others. Although Anglicans, for example, have agreed with the Reformed that, "the presidency of the ordained person does not depend upon his possessing a priesthood which others lack; it depends upon the good ordering which is essential to the life of the church as it exercises corporately the priesthood given to it by the one who is alone the good High Priest,"[19] the fact that, within Reformed churches, "good ordering" is a function of the councils of the church rather than an individual bishop suggests it will be expressed differently. Although some of the reasoning may lie in different understandings of ministerial priesthood which have arisen since the Reformation, this also accounts for the readiness in the United Reformed Church to ". . . make provision through district councils . . . for the recognition of certain members . . . normally deaconesses, elders or accredited lay preachers . . . to preside at . . . Communion services where pastoral necessity so requires."[20] Anglicans acknowledge such pastoral necessity, at least in bilateral conversations,[21] although not enacted.[22] Presbyterians, in both England and Scotland, have long held to the tradition that only an ordained minister should preside, although have never spoken of the impossibility of so-called lay presidency. One commentator writes, "It must be admitted also that there was something of a tradition among some Congregational churches not just that in necessity a layman could preside, but that it was good that he should do so from time to time just to show that the church and not the minister

19. ARIC, *God's Reign and Our Unity*, 53, §83.

20. The Basis of Union, URC, *The Manual*, 8, §24.

21. "There have been and there still are situations where, because of a shortage of ordained ministers... there are congregations which must either have the Eucharist without an ordained minister, or else have no Eucharist at all." ARIC, op. cit.

22. The Church of England does make provision for lay people to conduct "Public Worship with Communion by Extension" in which consecrated bread and wine from a previous celebration of the Eucharist is used. For this service the explicit permission of the bishop is required.

really celebrated the Communion."[23] Whilst "This advocacy clearly rests on a misunderstanding, since it implies that it is the president who is alone the priest . . . thus [contradicting] the doctrine which it is intended to support,"[24] it does illustrate the Reformed conviction, paralleled by Reformed ecclesial polity (in both decentralized Congregationalism and centralized Presbyterianism) that, although there is one who presides at the Eucharist, such a person, although the "president" is never alone the "celebrant."

The understanding of authority in the United Reformed Church, and where it resides, thus affects its understanding of both who should decide upon when the congregation meets to celebrate the Eucharist and upon whether such a celebration may occur without the presidency of an ordained minister. Although many in the United Reformed Church would subscribe to the statement, "The general rule should remain that the president at the Eucharist should be the person who has, by ordination, received the authority so to preside, and the church ought to order its affairs in such a way that this proper rule may be kept,"[25] there are few who would regard lay presidency as impossible and who would not disagree with P. T. Forsyth's comment, "Independency [later known as Congregationalism] is . . . a lay religion, and its ministry is in principle a lay ministry. But in practice the ministry is set apart by two things— by the necessity of handling the Bible, and the duty of ministering it to the actual soul whose confidences it receives."[26] With most of English Congregationalism now part of the United Reformed Church, and con-

---

23. Slack, *The URC*, 32.

24. ARIC, op. cit., 53. Here the Reformed character of the Church of England is clear.

25 Ibid.

26. Forsyth, *Faith, Freedom, and the Future*, 173. Forsyth was not himself an advocate of strict Independency. "Each single church is entitled by the Gospel to no more independence in the great church than each individual man has in the small, where they are all members one of another." *Lectures on the Church and the Sacraments*, 6. Forsyth's reference to Congregationalism as a "lay religion" does not advocate the abandonment of "order" in the church; he is speaking of the *laos*—the whole people of God—not of those sometimes called the "laity"—the non-ordained, non-clergy. Similar confusion has often been heard over the "priesthood of all believers," confusing the New Testament concept of the church as a community of "kings" and "priests" (essentially missiological), with a view that every believer is, individually a "priest," as well as confusing the Levitical priest (Latin *sacerdos*, an offerer of sacrifices) with the New Testament presbyter (Greek *presbuteros*, often translated "priest").

taining, as it does, a ministry of elders—"ordained to their office"[27]—the distinction between the ordained ministry and the ministry of all the baptized within the whole people of God becomes increasingly difficult to define.[28]

LOCAL PASTORS

This distinction between ministers and the laity was further complicated for the new United Reformed Church by the existence of "local pastors" from the Congregational Union of England and Wales. Such pastors were non-stipendiary lay ministers given pastoral charge over relatively smaller local Congregational churches, now part of the United Reformed Church. Thus, the new church inherited a "register" of such pastors, which itself posed questions.

> Our concern for local pastors and lay preachers who are authorized to celebrate Holy Communion has raised the question of the significance of ordination to the ministry of Word and sacrament in the United Reformed Church. The ordination of elders too is in need of clarification and explanation.[29]

27. The Basis of Union, op. cit., §22.

28. "As there were in the Jewish church elders of the people joined with the priests and Levites in the government of the church; so Christ, who hath instituted government, and governors ecclesiastical in the church, hath furnished some in his church, beside the ministers of the Word, with gifts for government, and with commission to execute the same when called thereunto, who are to join with the minister in the government of the church. Which officers Reformed churches commonly call elders." Other Church-Governors, *Westminster Confession of Faith* (1647), Thompson, op. cit. Interestingly, *Westminster* does not follow the view, often associated with John Calvin and championed by some in the Church of Scotland, that both ministers and elders are presbyters—"preaching presbyters/elders" and "ruling presbyters/elders"—speaking rather of the elders as "commonly called," presumably to distinguish such officers from the "elders" (*presbuteroi*) of the New Testament. This may well reflect the desire to stress the parity of the minister of the Presbyterian party with the priest (an English contraction of "presbyter," *presbuteros*) of the Episcopal party in the debates in the churches of England and Scotland of the seventeenth century. Likewise, *Westminster* defines ordination as "the solemn setting apart of a person to some public church office," thus not restricting ordination to the ministers of Word and sacrament; and although "Every minister of the Word is to be ordained by imposition of hands, and prayer, with fasting, by those preaching presbyters to whom it doth belong," the imposition of hands is not specified in the ordination of elders ("Touching the Doctrine of Ordination.") In the URC elders are ordained by the laying on of ministerial hands; in the Church of Scotland no such rubric is given. See Sykes, *Old Priest and New Presbyter*.

29. URC, *Reports* (1973), 37.

> The United Reformed Church recognizes the ministry of local pastors on the Register of Local Pastors as auxiliary to that of the ordained ministry. They are called to share with ordained ministers in the pastoral oversight of particular churches or groups of churches, and may preside at the sacraments and at the church meeting and elders meeting in the churches they have been called to serve.[30]

However, as with the taking of Congregational deacons into the ministry of ordained elders, so these "local pastors" were seen as an anomaly in a national church seeking to express, and practice, one ministry of Word and sacrament. The General Assembly in 1978 thus resolved:

> The action by which the church has traditionally set aside men and women for the ministry of Word, sacrament and pastoral oversight is ordination; and recognizing that there are some in the United Reformed Church who are now exercising this ministry without ordination; accepts the principle that it is now appropriate for such persons to be ordained and therefore gives discretion to district councils to offer ordination to the ministry of Word and sacraments to those presently serving as local pastors in charge of local churches within the district and to ordain them.[31]

Very quickly, however, the growing shortage of ordained ministers, the increasing frequency of celebrations of the Eucharist (at least in some churches), and a resurgence of a form of "congregationalism" in this matter at least, made it clear that the compromise statement concerning "pastoral necessity" was in need of clarification.

---

30. URC, *Record* (1973), 17.

31. URC, *Record* (1978), 18. As with the ordination of those who had previously served as deacons as elders, those not wishing to accept ordination but officially recognized as "local pastors" were permitted to continue as such "at present," though the list of local pastors was to be closed "from the date on which training is provided for the auxiliary ministry" (later called non-stipendiary or self-supporting ministry). The union of the URC with the Churches of Christ in 1981 provided in many ways the impetus for the development of auxiliary (later termed non-stipendiary) ministry within the URC. Elders of the Churches of Christ were ordained to a ministry of Word and sacrament, unlike elders of the URC—"Since the scheme of unification is based on the premise that we accept each other as we are, those presently ordained to such a ministry in the Churches of Christ shall be invited to continue to exercise it in the enlarged church as auxiliary ministers." URC, *Reports*, 55.

PATTERNS OF MINISTRY

At the General Assembly of 1989 the Doctrine and Worship Committee had noted that it had received queries about the guidelines on lay presidency and how district councils were to interpret them. Thus, in the following year, *Guidelines for Presidency at the Sacraments* were presented. Although they were eventually deferred by the General Assembly,[32] they did reaffirm the traditional role of district councils, functioning as "presbyteries"—bodies responsible for the ordaining and inducting of ministers and for concurring with the calling and the demission of ministers—and acknowledge the role of the elders meeting as the "council" responsible for the liturgical life of the congregation in the observation, "These guidelines do not cover emergencies, but assume that in such circumstances those in the congregation with responsibility for worship, that is the elders, will ensure that proper arrangements are made for the conduct of the sacraments."[33] However, the issue of lay presidency remained, leading, in part, to the report of the following year.

This *Patterns of Ministry* report presented to the General Assembly in 1991 tackled the issue of presidency at the sacraments by addressing the ministry of those who were not, at least in some quarters, regarded as "laity" at all.

> We believe . . . it is now appropriate for the United Reformed Church to take a new step with regard to the local ministry of elders. It is that each local church, of whatever size, should be invited to nominate from among its eldership those elders whom the district council might consider and recognize as *presiding elders*, for a stated period of years, with authority to preside at all services of worship and meetings of that local church as need arises. This provision would then replace the clause in . . . the Basis under which district councils may give special authorization to certain persons to preside at the sacraments.[34]

The reasons given for the change included the observation that, despite guidelines available, district councils interpret the existing clause in very different ways, concluding, "To have a stated discipline but to have no common exercise of it is probably the worst position to be in as far as

32. URC, *Record* (1990), 26.

33. Ibid., 110f.

34. Patterns of Ministry in the URC, URC, *Reports* (1991), 119f. The italics are my own.

our integrity and our relations with other churches are concerned."[35] The report decries a situation where a company of faithful people meeting for public worship should be deprived of the sacraments "solely because an ordained minister . . . is not available" and—using language appealing strongly to a Congregationalist understanding of the church—asks, "If Jesus Christ is in the midst where two or three are gathered in his name, may he not be present sacramentally?"[36]

Finally, in seeking to justify the status of presiding elders, the report appeals to a concept of parity in ministry which, it may be argued, was rejected by *Westminster*:

> In summary, we see that ministers of Word and sacraments (stipendiary and non-stipendiary) and elders will continue to form the group called to the regular spiritual leadership of our local churches. We regard this whole group as within the presbyteral ministry, ordained to their service with a lifetime intention. The mixture of what is the resource of the whole church and what arises from local church life is true to the nature of the church in the New Testament. Our proposal that presiding elders be appointed follows our conviction that every local church should have regular sacramental worship with presidency properly authorized.[37]

This initial discussion-document version of *Patterns of Ministry* prompted the General Assembly to request further study on the "presiding elder" concept. This, in turn, led to the presentation to the General Assembly of 1995 of the substantive *Patterns of Ministry* report. This report, in giving serious consideration to the earlier proposals to have a presiding elder in each congregation, noted how the possibility of this ministry was "primarily as a response to the need for presidency at the sacraments, and only secondarily to provide effective and continuous local leadership." It also criticizes the earlier reports suggestion of a parity of ministers and elders.

> To give permanent authorization to some elders to preside would . . . have been inappropriate because it would have formalized a pattern of ministry which we do not perceive as normative but exceptional . . . It might be taken by our fellow Reformed Christians to imply a change in our view of the distinctive characteristics of the ministry of Word and sacraments.[38]

35. Ibid.

36. Ibid.

37. Patterns of Ministry in the URC, op. cit.

38. Patterns of Ministry, URC, *Reports* (1995), 119.

Whilst the new report acknowledged that there are certain attractions in the view that ministers and elders share a common presbyteral ministry, it also acknowledged that this remains a matter of debate within and between churches of the Reformed tradition.

> The question of whether elders and ministers of Word and sacraments share a common presbyterate as ruling and teaching elders respectively, or are distinct ministries, reaches back to the time of Calvin and has been fiercely debated throughout the history of the Reformed tradition. It should be noted that the Scottish and English traditions of Presbyterianism never considered presidency at the sacraments as part of the ministry of the eldership.[39]

A "pattern of presidency" was agreed which, whilst affirming the original statement concerning "pastoral necessity" from the Basis of Union, also acknowledged the problems arising in situations of emergency. The Assembly also, therefore, requested the Mission Council,[40] "to consider the desirability of a constitutional amendment to ensure that in an emergency the assembled congregation may appoint a person to preside at the celebration of the sacrament."[41] It was this "desirability" which led to the resolution of 1998.

PASTORAL NECESSITY

As has been observed, the statement concerning "pastoral necessity" made at the union of 1972 was itself an act of compromise between those who believed that presidency at the sacraments was to be restricted to those ordained to the ministry of Word and sacrament, and those who believed that the church (for some the local church) could and should invite whomever it chose. The various debates at and reports to the General Assembly all sought to find ways in which these two traditions could remain together in the one united church. Furthermore, the district councils—the council of the church charged with giving permission for others to preside—continued to take different views as to what constituted a pastoral necessity.

---

39. Ibid.

40. The Mission Council is not a council of the URC. It is not unlike an executive committee of the General Assembly, acting on its behalf when the Assembly is not sitting.

41. URC, *Record* (1995), 45.

For example, in the council of the Chiltern district in which I served (1989–96) the then tradition was that permission to preside was only given for specific celebrations, when not only the date but also the time of the service was given, and when no ordained minister who was a member of the district council was able to attend. By contrast, in the Cambridge district in which I also served (1997–2008) permission was often given to individual lay persons to preside at the sacraments in a local church for a period of considerable months, sometimes years, especially in local churches that were facing an interregnum. Indeed, it was the actions of the Cambridge district council in 1997 that brought the matter to a head and, in turn, contributed to some of the clarifications (and new resolutions) brought to the General Assembly. I include this incident not only because I was present and involved, but also because the subsequent synod debate was but a few months before the General Assembly of 1998.

At its meeting on 28 April 1997 the Cambridge district council approved the proposal to authorize two of its members, both lay preachers, to preside at the Eucharist in two local churches "on occasions of pastoral necessity until the end of 1999."[42] This prompted an elder of St Columba's Church, Cambridge, of which I was the minister, to appeal to the synod of the Eastern province against the decision—an appeal he was entitled to make according to the Basis of Union of the United Reformed Church.[43] The grounds of the appeal were as follows:

> . . . that the Basis of Union . . . lays down that certain recognized persons, apart from ordained ministers, "may be invited by local churches to preside at baptismal and Communion services where *pastoral necessity* so requires;"
>
> that in the "Composition and Structure of the Councils of the United Reformed Church" it is provided . . . that it is the function of the district council, "in consultation with the local churches concerned and the moderator of the synod, to give authority for appropriate lay persons to preside at the sacraments;"
>
> that though in 1991 the General Assembly received a *Statement on Presidency at the Sacraments* . . . and commended it to districts

---

42. Minute 6.3. Council of the Cambridge district of the URC, 28 April 1997. These and subsequent minutes pertaining to this case are deposited at Westminster College, Cambridge.

43. Rules of Procedure on Appeals, URC, *The Manual*, C6.

... no substantive decision has so far been taken to alter the Basis of Union so far as this matter is concerned;

that the United Reformed Church, the constituent elements of which represent three distinct understandings of the church and ministry, has attempted in its founding documents to accommodate and reconcile these traditions and beliefs; and that the process of growing together can go ahead only if the Basis of Union is regarded as a covenant within which each of the participants respects the others' deeply-held convictions, and not a constitution where simple majority votes prevail;

that in particular the United Reformed Church includes members who believe that it should be an exclusively ministerial commission to celebrate the Eucharist and to baptize, and those who do not; and that the reference to "pastoral necessity" is an attempt to reconcile these conflicting positions, which both must honestly respect;

that therefore, while I accept the principle of authorizing lay presidency, an authorization given to preside at the sacraments which (i) lasts unbroken for two and a half years, (ii) is given in respect of two pastorates in which ordained ministers of Word and sacraments are already placed, and (iii) pays no regard whatever to the availability of ordained ministers within the bounds of the district at any time during that long period, though the council is aware that many ministers not in pastoral charge are currently resident within its area, not to mention numerous ordained ministers of other churches, cannot reasonably be understood as being given in cases of "pastoral necessity," grossly abuses the compromise on this sensitive matter set out carefully in the Basis of Union, and is a stumbling-block to those members of the United Reformed Church who cannot in their consciences regard such action as acceptable.[44]

The minutes of the synod record the arguments presented by both sides in the appeal, including the argument, "Essential to our belief in the holy catholic and apostolic church, presidency at the sacraments is, except in exceptional circumstances and only when pastoral necessity requires, a divine commission given to ministers of the Word and sacraments at ordination, and to no-one else."[45] After a lengthy debate, a vote was taken (in which members of the Cambridge district council could not

---

44. Appeal made to the Synod of the Eastern Province of the URC by W. R. McKay, 11 October 1997.

45. Minute 97/33, Synod of the Eastern province of the URC, 11 October 1997.

participate)—the result being a draw. With the moderator refusing to use a casting vote, it was agreed that the matter be referred to the Provincial Life and Business Committee.[46]

The pastoral concerns and the theological issues raised in the two *Patterns of Ministry* reports and the tensions produced by them—evidenced by this incident from the Cambridge district—all contributed towards the decision of the General Assembly of 1998 for "a suitable person to preside at the celebration of the sacrament in a case of emergency." What is at question is not who should be suitable. Once the decision had been made to permit lay persons to preside at the sacraments whether such persons are lay preachers, elders, or some other office holders, is a matter of degree rather than kind. And, as has been observed—and was acknowledged by the appellant in the Cambridge case—from its very beginning the United Reformed Church, in respecting the two different and differing traditions which first brought it into being, has carefully sought to balance the pastoral needs of individual congregations with its desire to maintain an ordered ministry of Word and sacrament. Such a desire is well summarized in the final accepted version of *Patterns of Ministry*:

> Baptism and the Lord's Supper are Christ's gifts to the church. Each in a unique way signifies and re-enacts the appropriation of Christ's saving work for his people. Those who preside when these sacraments are celebrated link congregations together in a common intention. That means that those who are baptized and admitted to Communion in one place are gladly received in other places too. Thus two principles should guide us in this perplexing and sensitive area. First, the sacraments belong to the *whole Church* as Christ's gift. Secondly, we must be *sensitive* to the ecumenical dimension of the way in which we order our sacramental life. The first principle means that no congregation should ever be deprived of the sacraments, and that there must always be someone available and authorized to preside. The second principle implies that those normally authorized to preside should be ministers to Word and sacraments.[47]

46. There was some irony in the fact that the same synod was being attended by representatives from the Congregational Union of Scotland, observing how the "councils of the church" functioned, prior to union with the URC.

47. URC, *Reports* (1995), 124–5.

However, the recommendation brought to the Assembly of 1997 and approved as a constitutional change to the Basis of Union in 1998, appears to change the understanding of authority and order in this Reformed church.

CONCLUSIONS

As has been seen, the general principle remained within the United Reformed Church that it is the function of ordained ministers, among other things, to preside at the sacraments. The General Assembly, however, now believes it appropriate to ensure that, in extreme circumstances, when the stark choice faced is between ordained ministry and celebrating the sacrament, the desire to celebrate may prevail. The fact that the authority to make such a decision is given now "in an emergency" to the local church meeting illustrates the way in which the conciliar nature of the national church has developed and changed.

Whereas some of a previous generation may well have seen such a resolution as an attempt to retain a rigid Congregationalist independency in the face of a perceived growing Presbyterianism, now it is presented as simply holding together one diverse yet united church. However, it is clearly a change, as it now gives, in an emergency, authority to a "council of the church" (the church meeting of a local congregation) to decide who should preside at celebrations of the Eucharist. Lest there should be any doubt as to the meaning of this decision, a proposed amendment to the resolution, to add the words "convened without such notice as is usual in that local church" to the phrase "The provisions do not prevent the congregation assembled… from themselves appointing, as a church meeting, a suitable person to preside" was deemed to be unnecessary on the grounds that, ". . . the words 'a church meeting' refer not to business meetings of a local church but to the classical sense in which 'a church meeting' can mean a church meeting for worship."[48] Whatever the position taken on lay presidency, this novel understanding of the "church meeting"—not convened by the minister (or interim moderator) as a "council of the church" but simply as a meeting for worship that may take to itself judicial functions—is a significant change. Not only does it give to the church meeting authority over ensuring the proper conduct of public worship—reserved in the Basis of Union, and reaffirmed in the

48. URC, *Record* (1997), 26.

guidelines of 1990, to the elders meeting[49]—it also redefines the church meeting.

Such a decision, I would suggest, is also inconsistent with an understanding of the status of the district councils of the church as the ordaining bodies. In a manner not dissimilar to the "presbyteries" of the former Presbyterian Church of England and still in the Church of Scotland, the district councils are (or were) responsible for the ordaining (and subsequent induction) of ministers of Word and sacrament. As such, it is to these councils—the "ordaining" councils[50]—that the General Assembly gave the authority similarly to decide when it is appropriate "in cases of pastoral necessity" to depart from the normal pattern of ministry. In a not dissimilar manner, it is the Conference of the Methodist Church that gives authorization to lay persons (invariably local preachers and not-yet-ordained probationary ministers) to preside at the Eucharist because it is the Conference that ordains ministers of Word and sacrament in the Methodist Church. Likewise, although not sanctioning lay presidency, it is the bishop in the Church of England who gives his license to ministers—both deacons and priests—to exercise their ministry within his diocese because it is the function and order of bishops to ordain such ministers.[51] It is from this Reformed version of order which the United Reformed Church appears to have departed by separating the "form" (what is professed to be the legitimate authority of district councils) from the "matter" (the new authority given to the church meeting, newly defined).

---

49. Among the functions of the elders meeting is listed, "to see that public worship is regularly offered and the sacraments are duly administered." URC, *The Manual*, B3. This is not dissimilar to the functions of the kirk session in the former Presbyterian Church of England. Of the fourteen functions listed in *The Manual* for the church meeting, not one makes reference to worship or the sacraments.

50. It is for this reason that ministers of the Presbyterian Church of England were deemed to be members not of local congregations but of presbyteries. Likewise, although the General Assembly of 1985 affirmed that "the names of... ministers should be recorded on the roll of members of the church(es) to which they minister," it did not specify that such recording implied membership, noting "ministers inducted to URC pastorates are... under the oversight not of the local church but of the district council" and "in full fellowship with the local church(es) to which they minister". URC, *Record*, 23.

51. Green, *Lay Presidency at the Eucharist*, and Church of England, *Eucharistic Presidency*.

This reversion to a more "congregationalist" understanding of the church is reinforced by more recent decisions of the United Reformed Church.[52] The *de facto* abolition of district councils and their authority now exercised by provincial and (for Scotland and Wales) national synods—whose effectiveness is questioned both by their size and their infrequent nature—and the calling of the General Assembly only in alternate years, means that the only effective "council of the church" is now the church meeting.[53]

It has also been seen that the conciliar polity of the United Reformed Church affects the way in which the church both thinks and acts in relation to "presidency" at the Eucharist in a manner not faced by, for example, the differing polities of Anglicans and Methodists. The covenantal nature of the union of 1972 (as for the subsequent unions) sought to balance traditions, often in tension and disagreement, but always with respect. With the passage of time it is inevitable that such an understanding has faded as more members of the national church rightly think of themselves as simply "United Reformed". However, the covenantal nature of the church did preserve important aspects of the Reformed tradition. From the Congregationalists, an understanding of the gathered and covenanted community as the church in all her fullness[54]; from the Presbyterians, an understanding of the essential character of the ordained ministry—acknowledged in the Basis of Union's affirmation that it is only those "called to the ministry of the Word and sacraments" who are commissioned "to administer the sacraments" by

---

52. URC, *Record* (2007).

53. *The Manual* interestingly speaks of "four parts of the structure of the URC" whilst mentioning five "councils of the URC"—"(a) the church meeting and the elders meeting of each local church; (b) the council of each district . . . ; (c) the synod of each province . . . ; (d) the General Assembly of the United Reformed Church." Such an anomaly may be accounted by a failure to agree on what is the "council of the church" in each congregation, the "church meeting" (from Congregationalism) or the "elders meeting" (the successor to the "kirk session" of Presbyterianism). Some see an intentionally Presbyterian character for the URC, at least at the time of the 1972 union, expressed in the statement, "The General Assembly, which shall embody the unity of the URC and act as the central organ of its life and the final authority, under the Word of God and the promised guidance of the Holy Spirit, in all matters of doctrine and order and in all other concerns of its common life . . ." URC, *The Manual*, B2–14.

54. This is far more nuanced than a post-modern form of "congregationalism" that would assume that "two or three gathered together" constitute a church. For the early Congregationalists such assemblies, rightly to be "church," needed to make a covenant between themselves and with God to form a community of saints in a given place.

virtue of their calling[55]—and the specific role of district councils (as successors to presbyteries).

However, such adherence to structure and order is sometimes presented as the antithesis of openness to the Spirit:

> The church believes that those who preach regularly in our churches and preside at the sacraments should be people who have been given authority through the district council; but this does not mean that we are to quench the Spirit when he calls men and women to exercise ministries outside our usual pattern. Above all, the church should welcome any disturbance of our pattern which leads to a ministry more ecumenical, more open to society, and more missionary in outlook.[56]

Few would disagree with a desirability of all churches to be "more open to society" and "more missionary in outlook." However, the suggestion that to adhere to the authority of the church's councils is, or may be, to "quench the Spirit," expresses a tendency to resort to a dualism of spirit and matter, inward and outward, which the Reformed tradition has long resisted, and speaks against the need for the effective presence of an ordained ministry as an essential mark of the church, catholic and Reformed.[57]

To the need for an ordained ministry of the Word in the churches, P. T. Forsyth was explicit. He saw preaching as sacramental—the preacher receiving the commission of Christ so to preach.[58] The preacher, as pastor, would also preside over the church's celebration of the sacraments. As a Congregationalist he would have accepted, ultimately, the right and responsibility of the church meeting to order the church's public worship: an authority properly exercised and ordered. Whether Forsyth

---

55. The Basis of Union, op. cit., 7.

56. Commission on the Ministry, URC, *Record* (1975), 54.

57. "The one who presides does so, not in virtue of a different relationship to the life of the risen Christ from the rest of the body, but because—as a matter of order—he has been so authorized . . . It is clear that this ordering is of central importance for the very life of the church. It arises from a genuine concern that what is celebrated should truly be the Lord's Supper. For order is love in regulative operation, and love is the fundamental reality of the church's being." ARIC, op. cit., 52. Subsequent paragraphs make it clear that the authorized order spoken of is that of the ordained ministers, not that of lay presidency. See note 19.

58. This is a central theme throughout *Positive Preaching and the Modern Mind*.

would have accepted the novel understanding of a church meeting implied in the 1998 resolution is doubtful.

Despite its claimed high view of an ordered ministry, the reality of lay presidency within the United Reformed Church means that ordinations have less practical importance. Elders serve as interim moderators of local congregations, lay preachers preside regularly in an increasing number of cases of "pastoral necessity," and church meetings deemed to be convened by the fact of an act of public worship—without a minister or interim moderator, one wonders by whom?—"in a case of emergency" may invite anyone to preside at its celebrations of the sacraments. Although the 1998 resolution makes it clear that such provision only applies in a case of emergency, as no full definition of "emergency" is given, there is no reason not to assume that as much confusion and disagreement over this term will arise as arose over the meaning of "pastoral necessity."

This essay does not address the current shortage of ordained ministers, faced by many churches in the West. Other churches have suggested other patterns—"local" ordained non-stipendiary ministers being one solution. Nor does it seek to challenge the practice of the United Reformed Church, of making provision for lay presidency. However, it does suggest that the current solution, of allowing "church meetings" (convened in a manner unknown to earlier generations) to permit such lay presidency resorts to a type of resurgent Congregationalism in keeping neither with the covenant nature of the 1972 union, nor with the predominant understanding of ordination and ministry within the Reformed tradition.

6

Can a Sermon be Boring? Metaphor and Meaning

Preaching in the Reformed Tradition

BY FLEUR HOUSTON

CAN A SERMON BE boring? The short answer, of course, is yes! We have all of us on occasion heard preaching that is dull and wearisome, sermons that lack the "vital spark," preaching that fails to engage the congregation. We may even have delivered such sermons ourselves from time to time! Advice on homiletics is readily available but what sort of a resource can we find in Reformed principles and practice? What principles and guidelines are available to us? This essay will begin with a discussion of Barth's theology of God's Word in the Bible and in preaching. This will be followed by a sustained engagement with the hermeneutical theory of Ricoeur, drawing from it some principles for the practice of preaching.

BARTH ON THE REVELATION OF GOD'S WORD IN THE BIBLE AND IN PROCLAMATION

We may usefully take as a point of departure the words of Karl Barth, the Swiss Reformed theologian who was arguably one of the most influential thinkers of the twentieth century. In his eyes, the answer is obvious, "For long enough, the words "minister" and "boredom" have been regarded as practically synonymous . . . If preaching is faithful to the Bible, it cannot be tedious."[1] But what does it mean to be faithful to the Bible? Barth prioritizes a particular doctrine of Scripture. As he sees it, to be faithful to the Bible is nothing less than to be faithful to the Word of God. And the Word of God in its written form stems from a divine act of inspiration, extending to all of Scripture. "Preaching, he argues, is the Word of God which he himself speaks."[2] What does that imply? For Barth, both Old Testament and New Testament witness to Jesus Christ: there is in the one an expectation of revelation and in the other a recollection of revelation. The subject of both is the same: the Word of God, the Word made flesh, Jesus Christ, human and divine. "One who believes in him," writes Barth, "believes in the Eternal Word of God."[3] Jesus' testimony in John 8.26 that the words he speaks are given to him by the Father is linked to the promise to his followers that ". . . when the Spirit of truth comes, he will guide you into all the truth."[4] In other words, just as the words of Jesus are divine words, through the leading of the Holy Spirit, the words of Jesus' disciples that find their way into Scripture will also be the words of God. In this sense, the Bible *is* the Word of God. Acknowledging, however, that "countless people would be obliged in all honesty to admit that there are large portions of Holy Scripture in which they have not yet heard the voice of Jesus Christ," Barth suggests that the Bible is best described as a token of revelation. But he insists, "there never has been a faith in the revelation which has passed by this token, a faith which was not revelation."[5] The Bible, then, belongs to the movement of revelation from God to human beings supremely realized in Jesus Christ.

It has to be recognized at this point that Barth's emphasis on Christ and the Word is exclusive. So much so that it denies God's "general revelation" of himself in creation and in human creatures, even though that also is attested in Scripture. Barth has no place for any theology that is based on reason and ordinary everyday experience. He cannot accept that natural theology has any place in revelation.[6] According to his understanding, people cannot know God just through being human and he has no room for the possibility that the Bible might affirm natural

---

1. Barth, *The Proclamation of the Gospel*, 93.
2. Barth, *Homiletics*, 44.
3. Barth, "Revelation," 63.
4. John 16:13 NRSV.
5. Barth, "Revelation," 68.
6. See Barth, *The Knowledge of God and the Service of God*.

theology in any way. His exegesis is similarly predetermined. How does this doctrine of Scripture impact upon preaching? "Preaching is the utterance, the subject and creative form of which is the biblical witness. As such it is a proclaiming of Jesus Christ's action as present ever anew."[7] Many people would agree with the substance of that, while recognizing at the same time that where there is no "point of contact"[8] on the human side, the proclaiming is bound to be less effective. Indeed Barth recognizes this to be the case from his experience. He writes bleakly to his friend and fellow minister Thurneysen on 19 September 1915, "I preached today with the clear impression that this cannot as yet get through to our people, even though a few, quite astounded, here and there raise their heads and note that something new is happening. It cannot get through to them because it is still far from getting through to me."[9] A discourse, however theologically sound, which bores its listeners may undermine or distort the intended message. Yet Barth appears to have given little attention to the requirements of communication and audience reception. We may deduce from this that Barth's doctrine of Scripture is in itself an insufficient basis for effective preaching. It is too exclusive; it does not provide the preacher with the means to make connection with her congregation. The proclamation of Scripture has to take into account the interaction of the Word of God with the contemporary hearer whose experiences shape the act of interpretation. A doctrine of Scripture must go hand in hand with hermeneutics. What we need, then, is a model that will bridge the gap between doctrine of Scripture and hermeneutics.[10]

THE HERMENEUTICS OF RICOEUR

At this point, we may find an important resource in the work of Paul Ricoeur whose hermeneutical philosophy keeps the conversation going in interesting ways.[11] Himself a lay preacher, a committed member of his local congregation of the Eglise Réformée de France, his work as a philosopher has an unusual affinity with theology. He has made origi-

7. Barth, "Revelation," 77.

8. *Anknüpfungspunkt* was a key word in the bitter and vehement conflict between Barth and Brunner in 1934.

9. Barth, *Revolutionary Theology in the Making*, 32.

10. See Watson, "Hermeneutics and the Doctrine of Scripture," 118.

11. See White, "Between Suspicion and Hope: Paul Ricoeur's Vital Hermeneutics."

nal contributions to exegesis and biblical hermeneutics. And he brings a comprehensive philosophical approach to the interpretation of texts. Although he takes care to distinguish philosophy and theology as disciplines, that very distinction can be mutually enriching. There can be productive dialectical tension between the two.[12] Ricoeur suggests that preaching is speaking God's text. If preaching is not just talk about God, but also talk *by* God, what are the implications of a human activity where God is expected to speak? The scriptural text may be seen as one link in a chain of communication: experience of God is expressed in the written text, which is then re-actualized through preaching. When living speech is recorded, as it is in the Bible, something is lost that has to do with the voice of the speaker, their face, the situation of the hearers. And when what is written is reconverted to the spoken word, a reverse process sets in and the text is open for re-interpretation often at a different time and in another place. Even if we accept the Scriptures as a whole as God's authentic speech, we still have to interpret them, we still have to deal with meaning and that meaning has to be faithful to the text. The model Ricoeur proposes has three stages.[13] He invites us to start with the text and with the way it speaks to us immediately—the classic fideistic approach where the reader draws upon subjective religious experience. But then we move on to the second stage: we are invited to make a critical examination of the text. This allows for form and redaction criticism, reflection on the narrative and its social context. Systematic theology too may be invoked at this point but only for clarification. None of these is to be allowed to dominate. The third stage points us back to the text, now a rich reservoir of meaning. New understandings and insights become possible.

A brief illustration might be useful. Let us take the words of John the Baptist at John 1:29, "Here is the Lamb of God who takes away the sin of the world." Following Ricoeur's model, we register our immediate reaction. There is a feeling of intimacy and love. We see before our eyes Jesus, God's lamb, God's dear Son, who died for us. And the imagery might be caught up in an instinctive movement of prayer, "Jesus, Lamb of God, have mercy on us." Holding on to that first reaction, we move on to the second stage. The image Lamb of God is rooted in Old Testament imagery. In the Servant Songs, for example, Isaiah 53:7, the servant ". . .

12. See Causse, "Reprendre et Commencer," 543.

13. See Mudge, *Rethinking the Beloved Community*, 114.

did not open his mouth; like a lamb that is led to the slaughter . . . so he did not open his mouth"; and in the story of the Passover,[14] when the people of God are set free from slavery, the lamb features as the cultural and liturgical symbol of Israel's deliverance. If we hold these two strands together, we have a rich deposit of symbols. And then there is the conquering Lamb of Revelation, the bridegroom at the marriage supper, who is enthroned with God, who is worshipped and glorified by those "who have come out of the great ordeal."[15] Finally there is the realization that Jesus does not just liberate us from our sins as individuals, he takes away the collective brokenness of the world. New perspectives begin to open as we return to the text, our first reactions now enriched by fresh imaginative possibilities.

Ricoeur's model has a significant contribution to make to the debate in three respects. First, it offers a balance between conviction and critique. He finds a way forward that embraces liberal and conservative approaches to the Bible.[16] On the one hand, he shows reverence for the given text.[17] He sees the New Testament in particular as testimony to the power of the Resurrection to transform the world. But he is opposed to what he calls "dogmatic mythology" in any shape or form[18]—interpretation of the Bible has to be in touch with "the great romance of culture." He challenges those who seek to make the meaning of the text clear and straightforward to find an approach that can deal with pluralism and biblical criticism; he invites those who readily accept pluralism and biblical criticism to take the biblical text seriously. Then, second, this model distinguishes the writing from the writer. The focus is not on what the writer might have wanted to say but on what *was* said. Ricoeur is critical of the tendency of some contemporary theologies to focus on the world behind the text at the expense of its narrative shape. And he is no less critical of those who deal only with the analysis of structures. The texts themselves refer to reality. They are rich in meaning. They project a world that may, or may not, coincide with the intentions of the author, a world *in front of* the text.[19] This world is available to others, hundreds of years

14. See Exod 12.

15. Rev 7:14 NRSV.

16. Stiver, *Theology after Ricoeur*, 77–8.

17. Ricoeur, "Biblical Hermeneutics," 29.

18. See Ricoeur, "The Hermeneutics of Symbols 1," 299.

19. See Stiver, *Theology after Ricoeur*, 92.

later and in different contexts. It has the power to refigure the world of the reader. For the preacher, this "world in front of the text" may involve a process of translation, of transference, of "dynamic equivalence." It is an approach that is often used in sermons where there is a particular desire to translate the stories of the gospels into contexts that the hearers can receive and understand.

Let us take for an example Matthew 2:13–18. The preacher may draw on verbatim accounts by contemporary refugees to describe Mary and Joseph in those terms—as a man and a woman fleeing for their lives, escaping persecution by a murderous dictator and a marauding army, seeking sanctuary with their baby in a foreign country. This is accountable to Scripture and is rooted in a concern to make the biblical narrative accessible to the hearers. In Mary, Joseph and the baby we see all innocent sufferers caught up in the destructive power struggles of our world, forced to flee from war, political conflict, or natural disaster. We have seen how Ricoeur's model offers a balance between conviction and critique and how it distinguishes the writing from the writer. And now, finally, Ricoeur's model recognizes that there is in the text a *surplus of meaning*.[20] Ricoeur's succinct statement "A text means all that it can mean" is not so far removed from the words allegedly addressed by Pastor John Robinson to the Separatist congregation in Leyden as they set off for Massachusetts in the Mayflower, "The Lord hath more truth and light yet to break forth out of his holy Word."

RICOEUR ON METAPHOR

For Ricoeur, the key to this superabundance of meaning is metaphor.[21] Metaphor is a way of knowing, a "paradigm of reality"; the knowing and the vehicle of knowledge are one and the same. Metaphors cannot be interpreted—they do not have a message, they *are* a message. We have already seen the force of this in the reference to Jesus as "the Lamb of God who takes away the sin of the world." Something new is being talked about in a new way. A "living metaphor" allows the meaning to be grasped without being totally explained.[22] The medium is the

20. See Stiver, ibid., 94.

21. Ricoeur's carefully nuanced system of hermeneutics is articulated most clearly in "Metaphor and the Central Problem of Hermeneutics," 165–81; and in *The Rule of Metaphor.*

22. See "Biblical Hermeneutics," 78–9.

message. It is difficult for us today to see how revolutionary this under-standing of metaphor was in 1972. For centuries, the use of metaphor had been perceived as at best ornamental, at worst disrespectable,[23] its use in preaching being chiefly as a rhetorical aid to communicating the substance of the sermon.[24] But with Ricoeur, the climate changed. He developed an interactive theory of metaphor, using the notion of "ste-reoscopic vision"[25] to describe the ability to embrace two different points of view at the same time. If we return to the metaphor of Lamb of God, we have on the one hand, the literal meaning, a young sheep, and on the other, the cumulative metaphorical references from the Bible. As these meanings are held together in tension, a new meaning comes into being, a meaning that cannot be explained but can be understood. Another dynamic also comes into play; for there is a tension between sameness and difference, which Ricoeur calls "a split reference."[26] As he puts it, metaphor says both "it is" and "it is not." A process of distanciation sets in—the text is removed from the original author, audience and meaning and acquires a metaphorical meaning and reference. It then waits to be re-contextualized by the reader or hearer.[27]

SOSKICE'S CRITIQUE OF RICOEUR'S THOUGHT

It is worth pausing at this point briefly to consider Janet Martin Soskice's critique[28] of Ricoeur's schema, which she finds "somewhat ambiguous."[29] She feels that his "approach comes dangerously near to making meta-phor a matter of comparison" and cites in evidence Ricoeur's "language of redescription" as implying that "there is some pre-existing thing that the metaphor is about and which it simply redescribes."[30] To make her

---

23. John Locke writes in 1690 of "the artificial and figurative application of words eloquence hath invented...for nothing else but to insinuate wrong ideas, move the pas-sions, and thereby mislead the judgment; and so indeed are perfect cheats . . . and where truth and knowledge are concerned, cannot but be thought a great fault." *An Essay Concerning Human Understanding*, Book III, §34.

24. See for example, Long, "The Distance We Have Travelled," 11–6.

25. See Ricoeur, *The Rule of Metaphor*, 87.

26. Ricoeur, ibid., 230.

27. See Ricoeur, "The Hermeneutical Function of Distanciation," 2–4.

28. See Soskice, *Metaphor and Religious Language*, 86–90.

29. Ibid., 89.

30. Ibid., 89.

point, she cites religious metaphors such as "Jesus is the lamb of God," which was not "intended by Christians as only an evocative way of describing an ordinary man . . . The phrases are not redescribing but describing for the first time."[31] In pressing Ricoeur's language too literally, she attributes to him a meaning that cannot be substantiated from his work as a whole. The intended sense of "redescription" is clear from his essay, "Creativity in Language"—". . . a discourse which makes use of metaphor has the extraordinary power of redescribing reality . . . If this analysis is sound, we should have to say that metaphor not only shatters the previous structures of our language, but also the previous structures of what we call reality. When we ask whether metaphorical language reaches reality, we presuppose that we already know what reality is. But if we assume that metaphor redescribes reality, we must then assume that this reality as redescribed is itself novel reality . . . With metaphor we experience the metamorphosis of both language and reality."[32]

RICOEUR ON PARABLES

One of the most important applications of Ricoeur's work on metaphor is its extension to the parables of Jesus.[33] Parables may be seen as extended metaphors, bringing together the secular and religious, "on a continuum with that time when the city of the world and the city of God shall be one."[34] The situations described in the Gospels are from ordinary life—sowing seed, harvesting wheat and tares, amassing provisions in a barn, throwing a net into the sea to catch fish, sweeping a room to find a lost coin, attending or hosting banquets and wedding feasts—but we are shown these ordinary situations in the extraordinary light of grace. The stories evoke the Kingdom of God.[35] The parables of Jesus provide Ricoeur with rich examples of linguistic extravagance. They enable a dialectic between what is strange and what is familiar, the remote and the near at hand. The stories are taken from everyday life, but they contain an element of the extraordinary. What shepherd in his senses would ever abandon ninety-nine sheep and search for one that was missing

31. Ibid., 89–90.

32. Ricoeur, "Creativity in Language," 110–1.

33. See Ricoeur, "Biblical Hermeneutics."

34. McFague, *Speaking in Parables*, 6.

35. Ricoeur, "Le Royaume dans les paraboles de Jésus," 31–7.

until he found it? What mustard seed would ever grow so tall that birds could make their nests in its branches? What host at a great feast would send his servant out into the streets and lanes to seek substitute guests? Such extravagance is disorientating, it stretches religious hermeneutics to breaking point, but in exposing us to what is unreal, it leads us to a new apprehension of reality. "The event becomes advent."[36]

IMAGINATION, APPLICATION, AND ETHICS

Recently I found myself talking with a class in the local primary school about the Bible; one child asked me suddenly: Are the stories of the Bible true? When I asked them if they knew any of the stories of Jesus, I was met with blank stares. So I told them as best as I could the story of the Good Samaritan. They were gripped. "But, Fleur," they said of the Samaritan, "that man was scum!" And then they remarked with incredulity, "He gave the hotel man a blank check!" And as we talked it over, the possibilities of the gospel came alive for a group of children who had integrated very early in their lives the feeling that they too were scum in a context where popular wisdom dictates that you avoid involvement with a scene of crime.

As we disengage ourselves from literal interpretation, we find new meaning. Meaning engenders meaning. New horizons open up continuously, and new possibilities unfold. Vision and revelation are kept alive. This is the poetic dimension of language. It is not geared towards scientific verification or indeed communication in any conventional sense but it has creative power; it enables us to discover aspects of reality that are otherwise hidden. We reach the heart of things analogically. Through poetic language, the great biblical network of texts engages us in its own world. Not a world of abstract ideas, but a new way of being in the world, of living, of feeling, and of seeing. The process is completed in the reader's imagination as she responds to the poetic discourse as a Christian. This then becomes constitutive of her whole way of being. And what is true of an individual is also true of the community of faith as a whole. Ricoeur calls this "ethical imagination."

Ricoeur sees application as integral to any thought. Praxis and appropriation for him are primary. His personal experiences left him with a horror of war. Orphaned at the age of two when his mother died and

---

36. Ricoeur, "Preface to Bultmann," 383–4.

his father was killed at the battle of the Marne, he was drafted into the French army in 1940 and spent the ensuing five years as a prisoner of war. During the 30s he had already begun to publish articles on pacifism. He was to become very vocal as a protester against the Algerian war; his bravery was greatly admired. In the 60s he wrote several articles criticizing the French university system and helped to found the new university of Paris-Nanterre where he was appointed Dean. It is ironic that in 1968 he was derided by left-wing students as a tool of the French government and felt obliged to leave the university.

The move from theory to practice is enabled by the use of imagination.[37] Imagination has bearing on our interpersonal relations and on the way we relate to our historical context. It helps us do justice to justice. It has an essential part to play in our moral and ethical behavior, what Ricoeur describes as, *"la visée éthique, visée d'une vie bonne avec et pour les autres dans les institutions justes."*[38] All our actions are focused on this one end, inspired by this one vision. How does this happen? First of all, we can, in our imagination, explore different courses of action; X might have certain consequences while Y might have other consequences entirely. In our imagination, we can also explore the motivation behind different courses of action. Both of these are indispensable preliminaries to making a decision. Then finally, in my imagination, I can test out what in fact is within my capacity to do. What is the role of imagination in solicitude and compassion? We might reply that this is something to do with our capacity to stand in another person's shoes; and Ricoeur returns again and again to this point.[39] Our lives as historical beings are bound up not only with our contemporaries but also with those who came before us and those who come after us. They think as we do, they experience pain and pleasure as we do, and we in our turn can imagine what we would think or feel under similar circumstances. The sufferings of other people, as they impact upon us, will arouse solicitude and compassion. What is the role of imagination in social institutions? First of all Ricoeur would say, it keeps human relations personal. It combats the anonymity of relationships in bureaucratic societies. It would otherwise be all too easy to become indifferent to the fate of those who are not

---

37. See Thomasset, "L'imagination dans la pensée de Paul Ricoeur," 525–41.

38. "Aiming at the 'good life' with and for others, in just institutions." See Ricoeur, *Oneself as Other*, 172.

39. See Ricoeur, *Du texte à l'action. Essais d'herméneutique II.*

included in our immediate circle of colleagues. But with the exercise of imagination, we can conceive of the irreplaceable value of each person, past, present and future.

Apply this to our own day and we may envisage an ethic of individual rights giving way to an ethic of the common good. Social systems, institutions and environments will work together in a manner that benefits all. There will be access to affordable health care, an efficient system of public safety, peace between the nations, a just legal and political system, and an unpolluted natural environment. In this way, social imagination feeds into a sense of justice; it keeps alive a sense of the equality of all humanity within our institutions. Amongst all the traditions that nurture this social imagination of a good life in community, for Ricoeur, the Christian tradition has an honored place. Mediated by imagination, biblical texts have a profound influence on the Christian believer. Thanks to the power of imagination, the texts educate our moral and affective sensibilities, and inspire our ethical vision, and our relations to our neighbors and to social institutions.

CONCLUSION

As we have seen, Ricoeur enables the preacher to appropriate the biblical text afresh. As she broods over a passage of Scripture, she will draw on the resources of personal conviction as well as the insights of scholarship. Scripture will come alive. New understandings and insights become possible. A new world comes into being, a world in front of the text. This has power to refigure our world. Through the exercise of imagination, we are convicted as if for the first time of the extravagant grace of God. We also have a fresh vision of moral and ethical behavior. This illuminates alike our interpersonal relations and the institutions of our society. Ricoeur describes it as "a call, a kerygma, a word addressed to me . . . To believe it is to listen to the call, but to hear the call, we must first interpret the message."[40] Under these circumstances, can a sermon be boring? Surely not!

40. Ricoeur, *Freud and Philosophy*, 525.

7

Holy Fear or Holy Communion
in the Reformed Tradition

BY DAVID M. THOMPSON

RATHER MORE THAN THIRTY years ago at the Church of Scotland bookshop in George Street, Edinburgh, I came across a leaflet about Holy Communion, which was designed particularly for churches in the highlands of Scotland. To my surprise the thrust of the leaflet was to reassure communicants that they could take Holy Communion without fear of damnation. I do not know whether this leaflet is still in print—probably not; it is certainly not available on the Church of Scotland website! But it raised a set of questions in my mind, which has never left me. They are reinforced by the situation in one United Reformed Church in Cambridgeshire, where I regularly conduct Communion. Notwithstanding that Communion is now an integral part of the morning service, at the point when we sing the communion hymn, about six members of the congregation leave. This seems to represent something quite deeply rooted in the Reformed psyche and the point of this paper is to explore it further.

CALVIN ON THE CENTRALITY AND FREQUENCY
OF THE LORD'S SUPPER

John Calvin's recommendation of weekly Communion in the *Institutes* is familiar. He wrote that "the Supper could have been administered most becomingly if it were set before the church very often and at least once a week."[1] His justification came in the following section:

> What we have so far said of the sacrament abundantly shows that it was not ordained to be received only once a year—and that, too, perfunctorily, as now is the usual custom. Rather, it was ordained to be frequently used among all Christians in order that they might frequently return in memory to Christ's passion, by such remembrance to sustain and strengthen their faith, and urge themselves to sing thanksgiving to God and to proclaim his goodness; finally, by it to nourish mutual love, and among themselves give witness to this love, and discern its bond in the unity of Christ's body. For as often as we partake of the symbol of the Lord's body, as a token given and received, we reciprocally bind ourselves to all the duties of love in order that none of us may permit anything that can harm our brother, or overlook anything that can help him, where necessity demands and ability suffices.[2]

Thus in the *Articles concerning the Organization of the Church and of Worship at Geneva proposed by the Ministers at the Council, January 16, 1537*, Calvin said that "it would be well to require that the Communion of the Holy Supper of Jesus Christ be held every Sunday at least as a rule;" but, recognizing that the "frailty of the people" was still so great that they might misunderstand it if it were celebrated so often, he proposed a monthly celebration instead.[3] In the event the council refused this in favor of a quarterly celebration.[4]

Calvin's reference to "the frailty of the people" is very revealing, though he might have been surprised to realize that this frailty has persisted for over 450 years. The particular misunderstanding to which he referred in the *Articles* of 1537 was the substitution of what he called "the sacrilege that one man sacrifices for all" (i.e., the Mass) for the "communion of the faithful."[5] In the chapter on the Lord's Supper in the

---

1. Calvin, *Institutes*, 4.17.43.

2. Ibid., 4.17.44.

3. "Articles concerning the Organization of the Church and of Worship at Geneva proposed by the Ministers at the Council, January 16, 1537," *Calvin: Theological Treatises*, 49–50.

4. See the addition to the "Draft Ecclesiastical Ordinances, September and October 1541," ibid., 66.

5. "Articles of January 1537," ibid., 49–50.

Institutes Calvin also spent several sections on the danger of superstitious adoration of the elements, and it seems probable that one reason why the question of lifting up the bread and the cup in the celebration of the Supper became controversial in sixteenth- and seventeenth-century Britain was the difficulty of guaranteeing that an action, the primary purpose of which was to make the elements visible to the congregation, might be misunderstood as adoration. Since there is never any way of controlling what people think in a service of worship, the simpler way may often have been to drop the practice altogether. The accusation of "idolatry" was always the way in which popular understandings (or misunderstandings) of transubstantiation were played out; and this was also characteristic of the ritualist controversies in the Church of England in the late nineteenth and early twentieth centuries. Nevertheless an eighteenth-century Congregationalist hymn writer, Isaac Watts, did not hesitate to write:

> Jesus invites his saints
> to meet around his board;
> here pardon'd rebels sit, and hold
> communion with their Lord.

> For food he gives his flesh,
> he bids us drink his blood;
> amazing favor! matchless grace
> of our descending God!

> This holy bread and wine
> maintains our fainting breath,
> by union with our living Lord,
> and interest in his death.[6]

The whole of Book III of Watts' *Hymns and Spiritual Songs*, "prepared for the Lord's Supper" and including "When I survey the wondrous cross" repays careful study for a sense of his contemporaries' understanding of the meaning of the Lord's Supper.

THE MASS: EARLY AND MEDIEVAL PRACTICES

W. D. Maxwell suggested that Calvin failed because the opposition of the people was too strong, and he traced this back to the time of Constantine, that is "from the period when Christianity became a popular religion,

---

6. Watts, *Hymns and Spiritual Songs*, 237.

and admission to it comparatively easy, without a long and intensive preparation."[7] Thus, although the matter was raised at several church councils, it was decided that the people must communicate at least once a year at Easter, and this became the general custom. Maxwell further suggests that, if asked why they took communion so infrequently, the people "then as now, would give the reason that Holy Communion was too high and holy an act to be entered upon frequently;" nevertheless such an answer "betrays an misunderstanding of what Holy Communion is and effects, and is entirely alien to primitive Christianity, where weekly Communion was the established practice."[8]

The extent to which Communion, as distinct from the Mass, was ever a feature of medieval popular worship has probably been exaggerated. There may be a romantic idea that the peasant in the fields would hear the Sanctus bell, and pause to remember his maker; but there is little evidence for it—not that it is obvious what evidence for this there could have been. Studies of popular worship in the late medieval period suggest that non-communicating attendance was the norm, except at the great festivals. The canon of the fourth Lateran Council, which laid down that everyone should take Communion once a year and which Calvin criticized so relentlessly, had always been a minimum requirement. But there is little doubt that the Mass had become an almost exclusively priestly affair, and the requirement that priests should say Mass daily made it more so, particularly in view of the development of masses for the dead.

ATTEMPTS TO REFORM WORSHIP AND PATTERNS OF THE ADMINISTRATION OF COMMUNION

The *Draft Ecclesiastical Ordinances* laid down that there should be regular preaching twice on Sundays at the churches of St Peter and St Gervais in Geneva (and on Mondays, Tuesdays, and Fridays as well) on the one hand, and the *Articles on Religion* emphasized the importance of the people singing psalms (led by the children, who had learned the music beforehand).[9]

7. Maxwell, "Worship in the Reformed Church," 131.

8. Ibid.

9. "Draft Ecclesiastical Ordinances," ibid., 62, 67, and "Articles of January 1537," *Calvin: Theological Treatises*, 53–4.

However, Calvin's comment about "the frailty of the people" is even more interesting, because it raises the question of how one can change—or "reform"—popular understandings of a rite, which in many ways is bound to continue to appear the same. In Scotland the battle, which had been lost in Geneva, was never joined. Although the *Book of Common Order* (devised by John Knox for the English exiles in Geneva, but published in Scotland in 1562) contained a rubric that Holy Communion should be celebrated monthly, there is no evidence that any serious attempt was made to enforce it. Shortage of ministers made it unrealistic in many parts of the country, and the *Book of Discipline* (1561) said that a quarterly celebration would be sufficient in towns and a half-yearly one in the countryside; but even this was not attained. However, this does explain why what became the standard frequency emerged. Nevertheless in some parts of Scotland in the mid-seventeenth century there were parishes where twelve or even twenty-four years passed without a celebration.[10]

Where there was a difference from medieval practice was in the way Communion was celebrated. From the beginning the emphasis lay on the congregation rather than the minister. This was most obviously symbolized by the early practice of gathering the people around long tables set up in the church, with the elements being passed from hand to hand. It was only in 1824 that at St John's Church in Glasgow (where Thomas Chalmers had been minister until the year before), the people remained in their pews, on the desks of which white linen cloths were laid, and the elders distributed Communion to them in their places. Despite being condemned by the General Assemblies of 1825 and 1826 it generally became the normal practice in the Church of Scotland as well.[11] This had been the practice in Congregational churches in England, probably since the mid-seventeenth century. Indeed there was a keen debate at the Westminster Assembly over whether the people should sit "at" or "about" the table. By "about" was meant sitting in their places, with the elements carried to them, as had been Zwingli's practice in Zurich. Whereas the Church of Scotland inherited medieval parish churches, which were not easy to adapt, English Independents, when forced to build their own meeting houses after 1689 were able to design them so that the pulpit and table were on the longer side of the oblong, thereby

10. Forrester & Murray, *Studies in the History of Worship in Scotland*, 40–41, 66.
11. Ibid., 42–43, 78–79, 83.

creating a space in which the people did literally surround the table.[12] Thus the fact that in the Reformed tradition the minister is typically surrounded by elders at the communion table is not only a functional necessity; it also helps to break down the idea that what happens in the service is the work of one person, namely, the minister. The emphasis on the communion of the faithful also means that it is expected that all will receive the elements—both bread and wine.

Although Calvin's influence in England was probably greater than some Anglicans preferred to believe half a century ago, it was never the case, even in nascent Presbyterianism and Independency, that he was regarded as model to be followed strictly. Many years ago Geoffrey Nuttall observed that the radical Puritans had a "more qualified admiration for Calvin" and a different center of reference.[13] For Nuttall this was the Holy Spirit; and he drew attention to the way in which the early Separatists from Barrow and Browne to Robinson, and even including Baxter, modified or denied Calvin's view that a true church was found where the Word was preached and the sacraments administered. Thus Henry Barrow declared that sacraments "were not a perpetual marke of the church;" and John Robinson emphasized "the gifts of the Spirit of Christ" rather than preaching and sacraments.[14] Such a view, combined with an emphasis on worthy reception (about which Calvin also wrote much) and the insistence that sacraments could not be administered until pastors or teachers were ordained in their office (derived from Robert Browne), explains why such congregations could sometimes live for several years without a celebration of the sacrament.[15]

If Communion was celebrated infrequently, it was nevertheless celebrated seriously. This may be seen in the pattern of the "commu-

---

12. Lovibond, "A Matter of Indifferency: A Commentary on the Cheshire Classis Meetings of 1691," 197–209.

13. Nuttall, *The Holy Spirit in Puritan Faith and Experience*, viii.

14. Ibid., 93–4; cf. Carson, *The Writings of Henry Barrow, 1587–1590*, 318.

15. I do not understand the logic of a remark of Clyde Binfield, apparently summarizing Geoffrey Nuttall's own view of ministry, that "the sacrament of Communion should invariably be linked to preaching on the death of Christ; this cannot happen with a weekly Communion." Binfield, "Profile: Geoffrey Nuttall: the Formation of an Independent Historian," 94. The second statement is a *non sequitur*; though it does explain why I had to change my preaching style, when Churches of Christ became part of the United Reformed Church. It took me some time to realize that the absence of weekly Communion had deprived me of the natural climax to my sermons.

nion season," which emerged in the seventeenth and eighteenth centuries. In November 1733 the newly arrived minister of Kinneff, south of Stonehaven in Aberdeenshire, James Honyman, gave notice of his intention to examine the parish. His catechizing lasted until February 1734, when he began a series of afternoon meetings for catechetical doctrine. From April to July he visited the families of the parish. At the end of August he announced that the sacrament would be celebrated on 29 September, and he would spend the intervening time preaching sacramental doctrine. He distributed communion tokens, entitling parishioners to attend, in the middle two weeks of September. A fast day was held on the Wednesday before 29 September with the preaching of two sermons, and young communicants were invited to speak with the minister; a preparatory service was held on Saturday at which they received their tokens. Two preparatory sermons were also preached on that day. On the Sunday morning the sacrament was celebrated, followed by an afternoon service. Finally there were two thanksgiving sermons on the Monday.[16] This was a particularly elaborate example, possibly influenced by the fact that it was the minister's first Communion in the parish. But the essential elements of the distribution of communion tokens after examination, a fast day in the week before, a preparatory Service on the day before, the celebration of the sacrament itself, and a thanksgiving service on the day after were characteristic of Presbyterians of all kinds, in Ireland as well as Scotland; and Duncan Forrester suggests that this pattern only finally disappeared in the 1970s in Scotland.[17]

The smaller branches of Presbyterianism had their own distinctive additions. For example, the Covenanters, and to a lesser extent the Seceders, expected potential members to express their adherence to the Old and New Testaments, the *Confession* and *Catechisms* of the Westminster Assembly, the Presbyterian system of church government, the perpetual obligation of the *National Covenant* of 1638, the *Solemn League and Covenant* of 1643 and the various *Testimonies* of the Covenanters, and to renew these prior to Communion. Sometimes Presbyterians prepared for Communion by making and renewing personal covenants, and the texts of some of these have survived.[18] This

16. Forrester & Murray, *Studies in the History of Worship*, 77–78.

17. Ibid., 181.

18. Holmes, *The Shaping of Ulster Presbyterian Belief and Practice 1770–1840*, 166–7, 176–7.

multiplication of subscriptions, going far beyond that required by the *Westminster Confession* itself, could be counter-productive. It was one reason why the Anti-Burgher Seceder minister, Thomas Campbell, an organizer of the Evangelical Society of Ulster in the first decade of the nineteenth century who emigrated to the USA, and discovered the same requirements there in Virginia, rejected all human creeds as conditions of fellowship at the Lord's table in 1807.[19] A similar urge led a Presbyterian of a different doctrinal stamp, Henry Montgomery, to question the right of ministers to exclude anyone from the Lord's table, even criticizing communion tokens on the ground that "the only tokens that God requires from sinners are penitence, faith and love."[20]

THE EMPHASIS ON THE "WORTHY RECEPTION" OF THE COMMUNION ELEMENTS

One of the points that Calvin and the Separatists had in common was the emphasis on worthy reception, though they came to it by rather different routes. For Calvin, it was important to take seriously Paul's warning in 1 Corinthians about eating and drinking damnation to themselves, but he rejected the Scholastic solution of "contrition, confession and satisfaction" as inadequate. Calvin believed that the worthiness required "consists chiefly in faith, which reposes all things in Christ, but nothing in ourselves; secondly, in love—and that very love which, though imperfect, is enough to offer to God that he may increase it to something better, inasmuch as it cannot be offered in completeness."[21] But "it would be excessive stupidity—not to mention foolishness—to require such perfection in receiving the sacrament as would make the sacrament void and superfluous."[22] Watts catches the point again:

> 'Twas the same love that spread the feast,
> that sweetly forc'd us in,
> else we had still refus'd to taste,
> and perish'd in our sin.[23]

19. Campbell was one of the founders of the movement known later as Disciples or Churches of Christ, or Christian Churches: see Thompson, "The Irish Background to Thomas Campbell's 'Declaration and Address,'" 215–25.

20. Quoted in Holmes, *Ulster Presbyterian Belief and Practice*, 172.

21. Calvin, *Institutes*, 4.17.42.

22. Ibid.

23. Watts, *Hymns and Spiritual Songs*, 247.

For Browne, Barrow and others like them, the significance of worthy reception was intimately related to the notion of the gathered or separated church. Both, therefore, condemned what they regarded as the indiscriminate admission to the sacraments in the Roman church; but whereas Calvin emphasized the need to treat excommunication with a new seriousness, the Separatists preferred a route, which would in principle render excommunication redundant by not admitting such people to membership of the church in the first place. This remained a fundamental point of difference between Presbyterians and Independents for at least two centuries. It was accentuated by the Church of Scotland's status as an established church, but it did not depend on that.

The tendency to read not only 1 Corinthians 11:23–26 as the scriptural warrant for the service, instead of using the words of institution in the Eucharistic prayer, and to add on verses 27–29, almost certainly had the effect of making people wonder what it meant to "eat this bread and drink this cup of the Lord unworthily."[24] I can indeed remember the thought crossing my own mind on more than one occasion in the years before I was baptized, when I was not receiving the elements myself. The Church of Scotland leaflet, mentioned at the beginning of this chapter, was certainly concerned primarily to offer the kind of reassurance, which is found in the passages from Calvin's *Institutes* just quoted. So where did the impossible understanding of Paul's words came from? Was it a deeply buried memory of a "catholic" past, or did it reflect the teaching that came from ministers less nuanced in their theology than Calvin, who really did want to make a point about the danger of eternal damnation? On balance, the latter seems more likely. It would be easy to question the depth of theological understanding reflected in such a view, but that would be anachronistic and unhelpful. What is more likely is that such teaching reflected the sense that puritan ideals were not being achieved, and desperation about what could be done. Thus the failure to win control of the Church of England was a disaster, because the separatism embodied in Protestant Dissent actually marked the defeat of the Puritan ideal. From this point of view, the history of English Nonconformity after 1660 ceases to be interesting; only the Church of Scotland stood any chance of creating a covenanted nation. Geoffrey Nuttall's citation of Ernst Troeltsch's dictum that "sooner or later . . . the sect always criticizes the sacramental idea" and "replaces the ecclesiastical doctrine of the sacraments by the Primitive

24. 1 Cor 11:27.

Christian doctrine of the Spirit and by 'enthusiasm'" has ironic implications for a sacramentally-minded Nonconformist.[25]

NORTH AMERICAN PATTERNS OF COMMUNION, COMMUNION SEASONS, AND REVIVALS

At this point a transatlantic episode is extremely illuminating. In 1749–50 Jonathan Edwards found himself in dispute with his congregation at Northampton, Massachusetts over the terms of admission to Communion, which eventually led to his dismissal. Edwards tried to insist upon a profession of true godliness on the part of those who wished to be admitted to church membership and Holy Communion. His congregation not only rejected his proposal, but also went to extraordinary lengths to prevent him even explaining the reasons for it from the pulpit. David Hall has offered a new and lucid interpretation of what was going on, by locating the heart of the problem in the quite different understandings of the two sacraments on the part of ordinary people in the early eighteenth century:

> Parents valued baptism for their children. They accepted the ministers' reasoning (or the ministers accepted theirs) that children within the covenant were better off because of being less threatened by the devil, more likely to obtain saving grace, and more apt to survive. Family preservation, the fundamental goal of the property inheritance system, was equally the goal of those who brought their newborn children to the church almost immediately. These people thought of the church as a place of nurture, a source of preservation and protection for the family. Yet the church was also a place where protection was intermingled with judgment and danger. Lay men and women regarded the Lord's Supper as encircled with this double message. Accordingly, they reasoned that they should not approach the sacrament unless they were assured of God's love for them...Lacking such assurance, and too scrupulous to feign conversion, such people harkened to the powerful warning of 1 Corinthians 11:27–28.[26]

25. Nuttall, *The Holy Spirit*, 92. Nevertheless it is fascinating that sociologists have generally taken Troeltsch's "church-sect" distinction (conveniently summarized at the end of Troeltsch, *Social Teaching of the Christian Churches* [English translation by Olive Wyon, London, 1931], 993) as normative with almost total disregard for the particular context out of which he was writing; and theories of church development which are ecclesiological rather than sociological are almost totally absent from the literature.

26. *The Works of Jonathan Edwards: xii, Ecclesiastical Writings*, 37.

This was a pattern which ministers found themselves powerless to alter; they lamented the number of those who stayed away, and were therefore even more reluctant to raise the threshold for admission. The onset of revivals in the 1740s encouraged those who had experienced assurance to demand stricter rules in the church. This was fiercely resisted by those of traditional background, who felt themselves under attack as a result of the very success of the revival. Edwards had gradually been changing his mind—Hall traces it back to entries in his "Miscellanies" in the 1720s—and it became apparent in his succession of books reflecting on the revival in the 1740s. Having first condemned the excesses of enthusiasm and defended the authority of the ordained ministers, Edwards came to feel that many in his congregation were not sufficiently sincere in their profession of faith. It is not surprising that they did not wish to hear this justified at length.

Revivals were an intrinsic threat to the Congregational gathered church, whatever the formal position on Arminianism and Calvinism. George Whitefield's influence was just as significant as Wesley's; and it was felt in Congregationalism and even in Presbyterianism. Leigh Schmidt's important book, *Holy Fairs*, has provided the missing link between Holy Communion and revivals by drawing attention to how often their origins can be traced to the Presbyterian "communion seasons," particularly those in the summer. The series of sermons, preached on successive days on the passion and death of Christ, became the context for spontaneous revivals. They can be traced back as far as the revivals in Ulster Presbyterianism from the 1620s, and spread into southwest Scotland in the 1630s; indeed Schmidt suggests that it was the strength which these revivals brought to Presbyterianism that enabled the Presbyterians to make a bid for supremacy in the Church of Scotland in 1638. More significant for the present purpose is his comment that "These evangelicals—pastors and people—had begun to turn the Reformed Lord's Supper into a popular sacramental festival."[27] In North America it was the same, so that whereas the Cane Ridge Revival in Kentucky in 1801 is widely remembered as the beginning of the camp meeting movement, it is usually forgotten that the reason for the camp meeting was that this was a communion season. Interestingly most evangelical historians have also neglected the sacramental dimension, despite the fact that it is demonstrated in so many evangelical autobiographies—Charles Simeon and

27. Schmidt, *Holy Fairs*, 31.

John Henry Newman, to name but two. But the evangelical revival spelt an end to the traditional kind of separatism.

What is more striking is the way in which these communion seasons were "reformed" in the early nineteenth century on both sides of the Atlantic. The driving force behind reform was a different side of evangelicalism, but once again one which had been there since the seventeenth century, namely a concern for moral order. The greatest asset of the communion seasons—their popular appeal—was also seen as their greatest danger. A gathering of a large crowd is by its very nature open to disorder; the opportunity after harvest for young men and women to come together in relatively unsupervised ways could have undesirable consequences; the tendency of people to move from the communion season in one church to that in another partook more of the nature of a holiday than a holy day. In so many ways the seasons could be described slightingly as "promiscuous." So the key to reform in Scotland and in the USA was to bring the gatherings inside the churches, where there was a natural limit to the numbers. An increasingly self-confident and unchallenged clergy could exercise greater control over what happened; and it is noteworthy that the earlier pattern was particularly popular in places where the number of clergy was limited, since parishes came together and the numbers made an open-air celebration essential. By the middle of the nineteenth century the old-style communion season was virtually dead, even though the pattern of services lasted another century. A move to quarterly celebrations, which was tried in some places, also reduced total numbers, in some places halving them.[28] The number of days spent was reduced from a week to often just one, and fast days also often disappeared. There is an interesting similarity to what the Roman Catholic Church did at Lourdes in 1858–59. The Pyrenees had long been an area where peasants had religious visions; these were usually dismissed as superstition by the Roman Catholic authorities. In the case of Bernadette Soubirous, she found a champion in a local priest, and the church authorities made a calculated decision to take over the vision and exploit it.[29] The rest is history.

28. Holmes, *Ulster Presbyterian Belief and Practice*, 191–2.

29. See Harris, *Lourdes*, 23–165. Acting on a report from the local priest, Abbé Peyremale, the bishop, Msgr Laurence, acted to channel popular belief to benefit the church as a whole (132). It was only after Bernadette was safely out of the way in a convent in Nevers in 1866 that the full exploitation of Lourdes as a pilgrimage center could begin.

COMMUNION AND CHURCH DISCIPLINE

Nevertheless more needs to be said about the significance of the discipline associated with Communion. From the earliest times exclusion from the sacrament has been the most serious penalty that the church could impose on those it wished to discipline. This practice passed into the Reformed tradition as well. In the seventeenth and early eighteenth century it survived almost intact, with the main emphasis falling upon offences related to sexual immorality of various kinds. The main difficulty in assessing the effectiveness of church discipline depends on whether one is looking at its effect on society as a whole or on those most regularly associated with the church. In the former case, it may be observed that church discipline alone was increasingly insufficient to stem such problems, particularly in the growing towns; as such it is an indicator of a gradual separation of many people from regular links with the church, except for those occasions when church involvement was more or less inescapable, such as baptism, marriage, and burial. On the other hand, it is not so obvious that for the church community the exercise of discipline was simply turning people away. In some respects a concern for discipline actually increased as a consequence of the evangelical revival.

This was most obvious among Irish Presbyterians. Andrew Holmes agues that "the reassertion of discipline by Presbyterian evangelicals had a significant impact upon the character of Communion."[30] The 1830s were the decade in which the evidence for this development is most common. Moreover, since many individuals declined to submit to this discipline and left the churches, it would appear that such discipline had not been exercised systematically before; and also that in a pluralist society discipline did not necessarily have the desired results. It was effective among the urban working and middle classes who were striving for respectability, but it was most effective in rural communities, which had not yet experienced the disruptive effects of an urbanizing and industrializing society. Church leaders insisted on the necessity for a purer church as a means to revival. However, there was continued reluctance at least before the Revival of 1859, to insist on evidence of a conversion experience as a prerequisite for admission to Communion. Thomas Clark, Burgher minister of Cahans in the mid-eighteenth century, had

---

30. Holmes, *Ulster Presbyterian Belief and Practice*, 192.

said that he was a Presbyterian and not an Independent because he admitted persons to Communion "with good knowledge and conduct," even though they could not "directly give positive signs or marks of their being converted."[31] In other words, membership depended essentially on the baptismal covenant. In the long run, however, this distinction became eroded. At the time of the 1859 revival several ministers observed that converts had had their religious feelings first stirred in communion seasons in previous decades. Thus communion seasons remained central to religious life in Ulster in the nineteenth century, despite the disorder that could accompany them.[32]

The Irish experience contrasts interestingly with that of the Free Church of Scotland after the Disruption of 1843 in Aberdeen. The city was unusual in that all the ministers of the established church seceded, which both created a severe problem for the establishment and also ensured ministerial continuity for the Free Church. However, the principal need of the Free Church was money for its Sustentation Fund (to support ministers). Since weekly offerings were still relatively rare, in the early years this enhanced the support of communion offerings; it was also a principal reason for the Free Church's inability to look after its own poor—the previous beneficiaries of communion offerings. From the beginning the Free Church (like the United Presbyterian Church, formed in 1847 by a union of the main Seceder churches) continued to exercise discipline; in fact, they were very active in the investigation of alleged offences by working class members, particularly those related to sexual morality and pre-nuptial fornication in particular. This could involve seeking evidence from employers to testify to their good character, and sometimes the investigation of others presumed to be involved. Where, as most often, this was a preliminary to baptism, in some cases the parents would rebel and have their children baptized elsewhere. Second on the list of offences was intemperance, and they even extended to walking for pleasure on the Sabbath. A girl who admitted taking a bolster or pillow from someone else living in the same house, was denied communion until further enquiries were made about her state of mind. On the other hand, middle class members were rarely brought before the kirk session for such offences; the main charges brought against them related to their conduct in business. In the light of this it is perhaps not

31. Quoted, ibid., 197.
32. Ibid., 193–8.

surprising that the Free Church in Aberdeen rapidly lost touch with the working classes.[33]

Although one might have expected that such activities would drive the working classes away forever, one interesting piece of evidence suggests the opposite. In the light of the problems posed by the growing city the Free Church in Aberdeen invested time and effort in the establishment of missions in working-class areas. One perpetual cause of tension between these missions and the presbytery concerned the right to administer Communion. The underlying issue, of course, concerned possible infringement of the rights of other ministers in the city. They centered on three missions, one involving a successful evangelical lay preacher and catechist, Alexander Laing, in the missions of Jack's Brae and Northfield, and the other involving the Gallowgate mission. All were successful in attracting large congregations of working class people. In the first case, the presbytery never agreed to permit Communions to be held at Jack's Brae, and only latterly did they agree to them at Northfield, not long before Laing retired. At Gallowgate the Reverend Thomas Brown was in charge (thereby avoiding the problem that Laing was not a minister) and Communions were permitted; but when the presbytery was dilatory in agreeing that the mission be raised to the status of a regular charge, they were horrified to discover that Brown resigned and took his congregation off to the United Presbyterians. The point of referring to these two incidents is not primarily to illuminate the internal problems of the Free Church (which they do very well), but to note the significance of the fact that all these missions were in working class areas, where there was clearly a demand for the celebration of Communion. So the sacrament still retained its significance for such people, but at the traditional frequency.[34]

One final point may be made before leaving Scotland. In the later nineteenth century various Commissions, either of the state or the churches, reflected on the morals and religious condition of the working classes, focusing particularly on the problems of marriage and premarital sexual relations. The Royal Commission on the Marriage Laws of England, Scotland and Ireland was set up in 1865. Among those who gave evidence was a Dr Strahan, who had a large midwifery practice at Dollar, east of Stirling, in Clackmannanshire. He had made a study of

---

33. MacLaren, *Religion and Social Class*, 121–31.
34. Ibid., 167–79.

parish registers and concluded that among agricultural laboring families nine out of ten women were pregnant or already had a child at the time of their marriage. He attributed this to their courtship habits, and what was called "night courtship", which was the result of the fact that parents would not allow their daughter to meet young men in the day-time but apparently had no objection to night courtship. Moreover the clergy either did not know about this, or if they did preferred to turn a blind eye.[35]

The Church of Scotland's Commission on the Religious Condition of the People reported to the General Assembly between 1891 and 1898. Both the north east and the south west had high rates of illegitimacy (i.e., between 14% and 17%); the percentage of illegitimate children baptized in rural parishes was significantly higher than in town parishes, and the percentage of baptized illegitimate children whose mothers were communicants was also higher in the rural parishes. Moreover the small percentage of illegitimate children baptized in town parishes was due to the reluctance of mothers to submit to the discipline of the session. The result was that such children were either baptized in churches, which did not insist on such discipline, or were not baptized at all. (The percentage of illegitimate children was lowest in the Highlands and Islands.)[36] Again the principal point to be made here does not concern sexual practice, but the wish even of those who had transgressed the church's moral expectations to have their children baptized or to receive Communion.

The attempts of the various parts of the Reformed tradition to square the circle of the tension between Communion and discipline may be summed up by quoting the pattern for the Minister's address before Communion in the Presbyterian Church of England's *Directory for the Public Worship of God* of 1894:

> in the Name of Christ, I do, on the one part, solemnly warn all such as are ignorant, scandalous, profane, or that live in any sin or offence against their knowledge or conscience, that they presume not to come to the holy table, inasmuch as he that eateth and drinketh unworthily eateth and drinketh judgment unto himself. On the other part, I do, in an especial manner, invite and encourage all that labor under the sense of the burden of their sins and fear of wrath, and desire to reach out unto a greater progress in grace that yet they can attain unto, to come to the

35. Boyd, *Scottish Church Attitudes to Sex, Marriage and the Family*, 52–61.
36. Ibid., 106–17.

Lord's table; assuring them in the same Name of ease, refreshing, and strength to their weak and wearied souls.[37]

This may be contrasted with words from John Hunter's *Devotional Services for Public Worship* of 1880, which became extremely popular in Congregationalism before official service books were published. Hunter was minister of Trinity Congregational Church, Glasgow. Hunter's invitation to Communion (actually entitled "Address") read (in part):

> Come to this sacred table, not because you must, but because you may: come to testify, not that you are righteous, but that you sincerely love our Lord Jesus Christ, and desire to be his true disciples: come, not because you are strong, but because you are weak; not because you have any claim on heaven's rewards, but because in your frailty and sin you stand in constant need of heaven's mercy and help: come, not to express an opinion, but to seek a Presence and pray for a Spirit.[38]

HOLY FEAR OR HOLY COMMUNION?

It is impossible to avoid the view that the more Communion has been linked to church discipline and presented as a conditional privilege, the more it has been surrounded by contradictory messages. If one wants to put it this way, its very function as an instrument of social control depends upon an acceptance of its necessity, which even in early times may have been less than the church was prepared to imagine; in more recent times it has lost its power in a pluralist society. Yet despite all this, it has been impossible to suppress completely the urge to celebrate. Schmidt wrote of the way in which evangelical ritualism extended to notions of spectacle, "of seeing the Christian faith enacted." So the Scottish tradition's premium on the preaching of the Word did not mean a devaluation of the sacrament; nor, as has sometimes been alleged, did the ear necessarily replace the eye as "the dominant sense of faith":

> The sacramental occasion all along represented a complex visible gospel. People came not only to hear sermons, but also to see them performed, not only to listen to meditations on the sacraments, but also to watch its celebration—the solemn procession of the elders carrying forward the elements, the careful Eucharistic

37. *Directory for the Public Worship of God*, 27–8.
38. Hunter, *Devotional Services for Public Worship*, 92.

gestures, the red wine poured out, the bread broken, the various actions of the communicants. There was undoubted spectacle in the all-day celebration of the sacrament, in the thronged meetings, in the tears of the repentant, in the ecstatic countenances or fainted bodies of the transformed, in the best clothes of the participants, in the brilliant white linens that covered the communion tables, and in the outdoor settings in groves, on hillsides, or in churchyards.

Sermons and meditations evoked the sufferings of Christ on Golgotha; taste and touch were involved in receiving the elements and handling the communion tokens. Although there were many words in sermons, prayers and exhortations, seeing and watching were always vital parts of this evangelical faith; "Word and sacrament . . .were combined in the rituals of these festal Communions."[39]

This is worlds away from the tradition in which I was brought up, and yet there are two important similarities: first, in Churches of Christ[40] Communion was a popular occasion, involving the people in a variety of ways and allowing for free prayer in the service; and secondly, full-time ministers were few. Ordained elders presided at the table, but in their daily lives they were identified with the rest of the congregation; often there was no significant social differentiation between elders and other members. The same was true of the Christian Brethren. It is a salutary reminder of the persistent tension between popular and clerical religion, which may well be particularly felt by Reformed churches. It is entirely right and proper that a special place should be given to those who are ordained to preside at the Lord's table, together with recognition of the significance of this vocation. However, that should not be confused with clericalism, which has to do with the exercise of power in the Christian community, which, like the exercise of all power, can easily become oppressive. The underlying question about attitudes to Communion may therefore be whether clerical religion can ever be popular.

39. All quotations from Schmidt, *Holy Fairs*, 216.

40. "Churches of Christ" was the generic name for the movement in the British Commonwealth; in the USA and countries influenced by it, the movement split into three streams known respectively as Disciples of Christ, Churches of Christ and Christian Churches/Churches of Christ.

8

Is there a Place for Eucharistic Sacrifice in Reformed Worship?

BY RICHARD HOWARD

To speak of sacrifice in connection with that act which Reformed Protestants usually call the Lord's Supper or Holy Communion can provoke strong reactions. And this is no wonder because the history of conflict between Christians can in many ways be identified with disagreements concerning what the church is doing when it meets to break bread and share wine in the context of worship. The notion of sacrifice in sacramental worship has been contentious in the history of the church, most notably during the onset of the Protestant Reformation. In his book, *Babylonian Captivity of the Church* (1520), Martin Luther attacked the practices of the Roman church, particularly the sacrifice of the Mass. In Luther's own words, "Let us . . . repudiate everything that smacks of *sacrifice*, together with the entire canon and retain only that which is pure and holy."[1] The enduring Protestant anxiety over eucharistic sacrifice has two main focal points. The first is that it seems to undermine the all-sufficiency of the cross in that if Christians are obliged to petition God constantly and repeatedly to act for their salvation through the Eucharist, then worship becomes an expression of *lack* of faith in the saving effects of the sacrifice of Christ on the cross. Secondly, the question of who is the *agent* in the Eucharist is controversial for Protestants. If Christ's sacrifice needs "activation" or "representation" by a priest, one might conclude that Christ is not as free and as mighty to save as

---

1. Luther, *Formula Missae et Communionis for the Church at Wittenberg* (1523). Jasper and Cuming, *Prayers of the Eucharist*. 3rd ed., 192.

the church wants to affirm. It is Christ and Christ alone who pleads his sacrifice. *He* is agent and initiator; never passive but personal, free, alive, and active. For the Reformers of the sixteenth and seventeenth centuries, belief in the Mass as a sacrifice transferred the agency of Christ to the priest, thus compromising the freedom and sovereignty of Christ and so had to be resisted at all costs.

SACRIFICE: A DEFINITION

The word sacrifice is worth defining because it has several connotations, some of which are more relevant to the present discussion than others. The word itself comes from the Latin *sacrificium*, which combines *sacer* ("holy") and *facere* ("to make"). So the root meaning of the word is "to make holy."[2] In everyday terms, sacrifice can be used to describe an act of giving up something valuable for the sake of something that is of greater value or significance.[3] For instance, a man may sacrifice his desire for a new car in order to pay for his children to go to college. In a religious context however, sacrifice usually refers to the surrender or destruction of something uniquely precious (e.g., an animal or a person) as an offering to a deity. This might be offered out of gratitude or in order to obtain some material or spiritual benefit. When reading the biblical narrative, a more specific definition of sacrifice emerges particularly in the Old Testament story of the near sacrifice of Isaac by his father Abraham.[4] In this event, which became so crucial to the self-understanding of Israel as the people of God, the sacrificial victim is not only Abraham's son but also the subject of a divine promise[5] and so his destruction would be a sacrifice indeed. But in this example, the deity (YHWH) intervenes and calls off the sacrifice providing a *substitute* victim—a ram. As a working definition for this discussion, let us consider sacrifice to be the outward expression of some transaction between human beings and a deity that affects the inner state of the human beings in their relationship to the world and its goods.

2. See the discussion of sacrifice in James, *Sacrifice and Sacrament.*
3. "Sacrifice." Soanes and Stevenson, *Concise Oxford Dictionary*, 1264.
4. See Gen 22.
5. See Gen 18:9–14.

EARLY HISTORY AND DEVELOPMENT OF "SACRIFICE"
IN THE EUCHARIST

In *The Manual* of the United Reformed Church, we read, "in obedience to the Lord's command his people show forth his *sacrifice* on the cross by the bread broken and the wine outpoured for them to eat and drink." It continues, "united with him [Jesus Christ] and with the whole church on earth and in heaven, his people gathered at his table present their *sacrifice* of thanksgiving and renew the offering of themselves."[6] But in what sense do members of the United Reformed Church "show forth" the Lord's sacrifice in the Eucharist? And how do they "sacrifice" themselves? Clearly Reformed theology has within it an affirmation of eucharistic sacrifice and this merits further analysis. The notion of sacrifice in connection with eucharistic liturgy goes back much further than the Protestant Reformation. The early church appropriated various sacrificial ideas from Judaism such as the sin-offering of the day of Atonement; the sacrificial ritual of the Temple altar and the paschal sacrifice itself, which became closely connected with the death of Jesus through the institution of the Lord's Supper. These in turn had a profound influence on the Christian interpretation of atonement and the Eucharist.[7] The Christian document known as the *Didache*, which some scholars believe was written around AD 60, describes the Eucharist as a sacrifice on three occasions in the context of confessing sins before breaking the bread, ". . . that your sacrifice may be pure."[8] By the mid second century Justin Martyr had outlined a complete service of Word and sacrament, the backbone of which became known as the Eucharist, the Sacred Liturgy, or the Lord's Meal. Justin explained the origins of the Eucharist as prefigured in the cleansed leper's offering of grain[9] and prophesied in Malachi, where we read, "in every place incense is offered to my name, and a *pure offering*."[10] In this way, the Eucharist was explained as a cultic act[11] in which bread and wine are offered ritually as a "memorial" and a "thanksgiving." The idea of eucharistic sacrifice was developed by Irenaeus of

6. The Basis of Union, §15.

7. Brilioth, *Eucharistic Faith and Practice*, 42.

8. Jasper and Cuming, op. cit., 24.

9. Lev 14:10 NRSV, my italics.

10. Mal 1:11 NRSV.

11. An organized gathering of adherents to a particular religious belief (or set of beliefs) who collectively direct their attention to a shared object of devotion.

Lyon (125–202) in whose writings the bread and wine were clearly stated to be sacrificial offerings. "For we make an oblation to God of the bread and the cup of blessing, giving him thanks in that he has commanded the earth to bring forth these fruits for our nourishment. And then, when we have perfected the oblation, we invoke the Holy Spirit, that he may exhibit this sacrifice, both the bread the body of Christ, and the cup the blood of Christ . . ."[12] On the other hand, Irenaeus did not make an explicit association between the Eucharist and Christ's death. If the Eucharist is a sacrifice, it is principally a thank-offering not a sin-offering. And this is based on his wider theological conviction that God is characterized in all his dealings with humanity by gratuitous generosity and that the whole of creation has an inherent goodness.[13] We begin to see something of the theological breadth of Irenaeus' thought in that his understanding of eucharistic sacrifice encompasses not just creation, but redemption as well. The gifts that Christians are commanded to offer up in sacrifice are the first fruits of the *new* creation. All this provides a rich background to the language and symbolism of eucharistic sacrifice in the early church and without making it explicit, Irenaeus moved close to the image of Christ being offered in the Eucharist. For if Christians are called to be a priestly people, sacramentally enacting their obedience and gratitude to God and bearing fruit for him, then what they are offering is no less than the harvest of the new creation, that is the *humanity of Christ*, in which human nature is perfected and offered back to humankind.[14] The use of sacrificial language for the material gifts offered at the altar is reflected in the eucharistic prayer of the *Apostolic Constitutions* (fourth century), where it says, "Again we give thanks to you, our Father, for the precious blood of Jesus Christ which was poured out for us, and the precious body of which also we perform these symbols; for he commanded us to proclaim his death . . ."[15] Later, the elements of bread and wine are spoken of in direct relation to Christ's sacrifice: ". . . we offer you, King and God, according to his commandment, this bread and this cup . . . send down your Holy Spirit upon this sacrifice . . ."[16] Subsequent

12. Irenaeus, *Fragments*, xxxvii in: Roberts and Donaldson, *Ante-Nicene Fathers Vol. I*, 574.

13. Brilioth, op. cit., 45.

14. Williams, *Eucharistic Sacrifice*, 10.

15. *The Apostolic Constitutions*, Book VII. In Jasper & Cuming, op. cit., 102.

16. *The Apostolic Constitutions*, Book VIII. In ibid., 111.

developments in the liturgy made explicit the realism of Christ's body and blood being offered in the Eucharist. The North African bishop Cyprian (c. 258) referred to the Eucharist as "the sacrament of the sacrifice of the Lord" and explained the link between what Christ did and what the church now does in terms of Christ's Priesthood. "For who is a priest of the most high God than our Lord Jesus Christ, who offered a sacrifice to God the Father, and offered that very same thing which Melchizedek had offered, that is, bread and wine, to wit, His body and blood?"[17] Cyprian goes on to explain that when the priest imitates Christ in the eucharistic liturgy, he "offers a true and full sacrifice in the church to God the Father."[18] In his commentary on the eucharistic liturgy, Cyril of Jerusalem (c. 350) affirmed that during the prayer to invoke the Holy Spirit (the *epiklesis*), the bread and wine become the body and blood of Christ as the water was changed into wine during the wedding at Cana.[19] In these terms, the "bread and wine"/"body and blood" in the Eucharist was understood to be sacrificed for sins and God was propitiated.[20] However, John Chrysostom (c. 407) was careful to stress that the eucharistic sacrifice was the *same* sacrifice as Calvary, which is constantly offered in the heavenly and spiritual realms, a reality that actually renders all subsequent sacrifices unnecessary.[21] The "transformation" of the elements of bread and wine into the body and blood of Christ became a focus of attention in both the Eastern and Western liturgies. In the Western church in particular, emphasis was placed on Christ's words of institution at the Last Supper as found in the synoptic Gospels:[22] "This is my body . . . This is my blood", such that the words when recited by the priest were seen to effect the conversion of the elements.[23] From these observations, we can discern a trajectory within the development of the eucharistic liturgy towards a sacramental realism, whereby the offerings

17. Cyprian, *Epistles*, lxii, 4, 14, 17. In Roberts and Donaldson, *Ante-Nicene Fathers Vol. V*, 359–63.

18. Ibid.

19. James, *Sacrifice and Sacrament*, 209. See also John 2:1–11.

20. Propitiation: from the Latin *propitiare* meaning to make favorable. A propitiatory sacrifice appeases God and makes him favorable once again.

21. Chrysostom, *Epistle to the Hebrews*, hom. xiii, 3; xiv, 1, 2; xvii, 3. In Schaff, *Nicene and Post-Nicene Fathers Vol. XIV*, 428–33, 447.

22. Cf. Matt 26:26–8, Mark 14:22–4, Luke 22:14–9.

23. This view is found in the writings of Ambrose of Milan (AD 374–97) as discussed in James, op. cit., 211.

of bread and wine mysteriously *become* the body and blood of Christ together with the corresponding close connection between this change and the words spoken by the priest.

PROTESTANT REACTION TO THE THEOLOGY
OF SACRIFICE IN THE MASS

Among the Protestant Reformers of the sixteenth century, such as Martin Luther and John Calvin, a suspicion arose that the church was offering a view of the Mass close to superstition in that the priest's words and offering might be understood to possess in themselves a power to propitiate God in isolation from the sacrifice of the Cross. Luther, Calvin, and others sought to eliminate any prayers that implied eucharistic sacrifice except with respect to the unique work of Christ and the self-offering of the worshippers. In the classic polemic against the Mass, the Reformers argued that the only sacrifice that can be spoken of is Christ's original sacrifice on the cross, of which the Eucharist was a memorial, and the sacrifice of praise and thanksgiving offered by the worshippers. Luther's desire was not to rid Christian worship of the Mass but to purify it. He passionately believed that the church's celebration of this sacrament had acquired so many layers of tradition that it had been changed beyond recognition from the intentions of the first Christians and ultimately, Christ himself. The reason for Luther's attack on the Roman rite was predominantly theological. For him, the Eucharist was a "testament" conveying God's gracious gift to humankind; whereas he thought that the Roman church was turning the gospel of grace on its head with its eucharistic liturgy, expressing a sacrifice offered by *men* to God.[24] He strongly opposed the idea that the Mass was a sacrifice, whether as a *repetition* of the sacrifice on Golgotha, or an *additional* one. He also criticized the idea that the eucharistic sacrifice is an offering of Christ performed by the priest for the church. The specter of what Luther feared is well expressed by Gustaf Aulén, "[The Mass] denies that the act which Christ has done once for all is sufficient and that the sacrifice he has made is eternally valid. Behind [this] sacrifice lurks . . . God who must be propitiated by continued sacrifices."[25] Luther's own opinion on the relationship between Christ's sacrifice on the cross and the Eucharist

24. Aulén, *Eucharist and Sacrifice*, 65–102.
25. Ibid., 83.

is central to his argument. Although he rejected what he saw as an erroneous concept of sacrifice, his *Treatise on the New Testament* (1520) stresses that Christians should *offer* themselves and everything that they are in fervent prayer. Moreover, Luther affirmed the priestly work of Christ in heaven, saying that we should put ourselves *on Christ* with our sacrifice of prayer and praise for he brings these into God's presence. To this extent Luther accepts that there is a "continuous sacrifice" of Christ in heaven but maintains that "we do not offer Christ as a sacrifice, but Christ offers us. [Only] in this way is it permissible . . . to call the Mass a sacrifice."[26]

Like Luther and other Reformers before him, John Calvin disliked the medieval Roman rite, which he called "magical mumblings," and intended to recover the Eucharist in its primitive simplicity as the weekly worship of the church. He believed that an authentic service would "manifest God's glory and allow the sweetness of consolation to fill the hearts of the faithful." For Calvin, not only the vocabulary of the Roman rite was wrong, engaging the faithful in a misconception of what the Lord's Supper was all about, but also the symbolism was erroneous. He believed the processing-in of the elements, their placement on an altar, and their elevation as a sacrifice by the priest could lead hearts and minds into great doctrinal and spiritual error. In essence, Calvin believed that the doctrine of the Mass as a sacrifice could lead Christians into thinking that they could be the authors of their own salvation thus undermining the gratuitous grace of God. If a person could go to Mass when he wished and perhaps pay for many masses to be said then what place was there for the free action of God in his soul? Salvation would become something akin to self-help.[27]

Calvin's own rite focused attention on *union* with the risen and ascended Lord, expressing the view that the Eucharist is the corporate instrument of God's chosen people through which they receive spiritual sustenance and by means of which they are enabled to show forth his glory. Calvin identified three spiritual benefits that partakers gain through this sacrament:[28] it *confirms faith*, it *awakens our thanks*, and it *encourages mutual love*. Because we share in the one body corpo-

26. Ibid., 85.

27. See the extensive discussion of these issues in: Clark, *Eucharistic Sacrifice and the Reformation*.

28. Rice and Huffstutler, *Reformed Worship*, 69.

rately, we are made one with all who join us in that sharing: therefore the Eucharist is the ground of Christian community.[29] On the specific issue of eucharistic sacrifice, Calvin is as clear as Luther in that the only sacrifice involved in the Eucharist is the "sacrifice of praise, prayer and thanksgiving" offered up by the worshippers, "[which] has nothing to do with appeasing God's wrath . . . obtaining forgiveness of sins, or . . . meriting righteousness; but is concerned solely with magnifying and exalting God."[30] If we refer back to the definition of sacrifice worked out earlier, we can see that Calvin's definition concentrates on the "thanksgiving" aspect of sacrifice but does not consider how the eucharistic liturgy can contain the offering of a "victim." It is also not clear how a "sacrifice of praise" falls into the categories of our definition other than in the respect that the worshippers sacrifice their time and other interests in order to participate in the liturgy. We can at this stage also identify an important question less readily dealt with in the works of Luther and Calvin. This is the question of "offering"—not just how Christ's sacrifice on the cross is offered in the Eucharist but how Christians *offer* Christ as his body on earth and how they *offer* the world to God. From the thrust of Calvin's eucharistic theology one is left with the feeling that his vision is not wide enough. The Lord's Supper is not just about the unity of the gathered congregation, still less about the individual and his or her salvation with the Lord. There is a much wider, possibly more profound, and genuinely "priestly" responsibility to be undertaken in the Eucharist—nothing less than the offering of the whole world to God.

SACRIFICE AND MEMORIAL

One of the most fruitful products of modern liturgical scholarship has been the exposition of the biblical meaning of "memorial." According to this scholarship, memorial is not about "remembering" in a weak sense but about allowing a past event to become a present reality, with all its benefits.[31] The Eucharist is the *memorial* (in Greek, *anamnēsis*) of the crucified and risen Christ, that is, the *living* and *effective* sign of

29. Significantly, the Eucharist was also the *test* of Christian Community for Calvin, which he enforced with a comprehensive list of anathemas that were read out before the Communion Rite of his liturgy. See Jasper and Cuming, *Prayers of the Eucharist*, 2nd ed., 154.

30. Calvin, *Institutes*, 4.18.16.

31. Thurian, *Ecumenical Perspectives on Baptism, Eucharist and Ministry*, 95.

his sacrifice, accomplished once-for-all on the cross and still efficacious for all humanity. Christ, with all that he has accomplished, is present in the *anamnēsis* giving us communion with himself. The key word here is "re-presentation"—a word that can be ambiguous. What it means in this context is: "making present again," which needs to be distinguished from the other meaning it could have of "illustrating" or simply "standing in the place of." In the Eucharist the church gratefully recalls God's mighty acts of salvation, asking him to bestow the benefits of Christ's sacrifice to all people in the present, looking forward to the final completion of God's kingdom. The *anamnēsis* holds together these dimensions and expresses them in thanksgiving and intercession. In fact, it is the remembrance of Christ in the Eucharist that forms the basis and source of all Christian prayer.

From this it appears that the main issues concerning eucharistic sacrifice can be distilled to a need for greater clarification concerning the ideas of "re-presentation" and "offering." Also, the relationship between the sacrifice of the cross and the Eucharist remains troublesome. Finally, there needs to be an effort to resolve the tension between Christ's finished "once-for-all" sacrifice and the on-going nature of Christ's work. Perhaps there are ways of handling the language and symbolism of eucharistic sacrifice that do not violate the Reformed insistence on the priority of Christ's agency, whilst taking seriously the presence and activity of the living, risen Lord in the Eucharist, continuing to dispense the benefits of his sacrificial death to his followers.

A CONSTRUCTIVE THEOLOGY OF SACRIFICE
IN THE EUCHARIST

We have seen how in the early church the language of sacrifice was present in the eucharistic liturgy. For Irenaeus, there is a close connection between our *offering* of bread and wine, our *offering* of Jesus' deified humanity, and Christ's *offering* to us of the gift of risen life through the nourishment of the first fruits of creation. What Irenaeus expounds is a doctrine of God that is based on his gratuitous generosity. God is seen as sufficient, needing nothing from us, having within himself all praise and glory in the eternal communion of Father, Son, and Holy Spirit. And it is from the dynamic life of God as Trinity that he desires to draw all people to himself. In the light of this, a theology of propitiatory sacrifice, unless very carefully formulated, could lead us in the wrong direction. It is far better to view eucharistic sacrifice as expressive rather than functional, making what Christians do in the Eucharist an expression of joy and thanksgiving. The offering of bread and wine through Christ becomes a fusion of earthly and heavenly realities, signifying the fact that God chooses to draw close to human beings through creation in the Word made flesh, thus imbuing the bread and wine with a new significance. Moreover, to understand how the church can *offer Christ* in the Eucharist it is helpful to recall Irenaeus' point about God's self-sufficiency and eternal communion of joy in himself as Father, Son, and Holy Spirit. Christians are given the privilege of reflecting and participating in what Father and Son do eternally in the complete self-giving of themselves to each other—"in the gratuity . . . of a thanksgiving which God does not need, we experience in ourselves something of God's own gratuity which is the giving of glory."[32] If we hold to the definition of sacrifice as the outward expression of a transaction between human beings and God that affects the inner state of the human beings in their relationship to the world and its goods, then we can view sacrifice as the necessary *ritual* counterpart to an expression of grateful love. And so it is possible to see a link between the church's earthly offering of praise and the eternal "liturgy" of the Trinity.[33]

The other enduring concern of Reformed theology is that the priest on behalf of the church does not offer anything in the Eucharist. Lying behind this is the belief that Christians cannot perform any "work" before God in their own strength that would reconcile God to themselves. In a sense this is true, but there is no necessary contradiction between Christian offering and the offering of Christ. There is no necessary contradiction in maintaining that the ritual offering adds nothing to the work of Christ whilst asserting its value, because the whole act flows from the prior reality of God's inner relatedness. "We do not work our salvation in offering the Eucharist . . . we witness to the share we have been given in the glorified life of Christ, manifest in the rest of our lives as charity, humility and pity."[34] Furthermore, it is always Jesus Christ himself, the true high priest, who is the offerer of the offering of himself, made once-for-all on the cross.[35] This is explained in the letter to the

32. Williams, op. cit., 10.
33. Ibid., 11.
34. Ibid.
35. Nichols, "The Holy Oblation," 267.

Hebrews, which insists that the "atoning sacrifice" can only be made by one whose priesthood is intrinsic to his very being—"Although he was a Son, he learned obedience through what he suffered; and having been made perfect, he became the source of eternal salvation for all who obey him, having been designated by God a high priest according to the order of Melchizedek."[36] Early Christianity, arguing that there is only one atoning or propitiatory sacrifice, used the Jewish symbolism of atonement—Christ's death effected on earth in the flesh and received in heaven. Because of this, and through it, Christian prayer and the life of discipleship are present before God at his heavenly altar. Therefore one may only speak of Christian priesthood in a derivative sense—Christians do not "offer" from a stationary starting point, but only because they are being offered by the eternal high priest Jesus and because they have been made a worthy offering by the atonement achieved through the cross. This understanding is beautifully depicted in the writings of St Ephrem, a Syrian church Father, who commentated on Simeon's offering of the infant Jesus in the Temple:[37] "Simeon . . . understood [that] when he beheld him . . . he was not offering Christ but was himself being offered . . . [T]he one who receives offerings gave himself to be offered by another, so that those who offered him might themselves be offered."[38] Interestingly, there is a strong parallel here with Luther who, as discussed earlier, could speak of offering Christ in the Eucharist inasmuch as Christians are offered. In this light, Reformed concerns seem less insurmountable, for there is no question of a "human" work undertaken in the church's own strength. Christians are already caught up in the dynamic action of God's grace. But we can go further and shed light on the other contentious issue, namely, the relationship between the sacrifice of the cross and the Eucharist. Again, the comments of St Ephrem are insightful—"In the presentation, in the Eucharist, and in the crucifixion, the agency appears to be human; but in fact all that human beings are doing in each of these instances is involving themselves in the divine action which presents them to the Father."[39] So the human agency of the church merely gives Christ the exercise of priesthood in the world in order to render his humanity as a priestly and prophetic reality. And

36. Heb 5:9–10 NRSV.
37. Luke 2:27–8.
38. Williams, op. cit., 14.
39. Ibid., 22.

this is certainly a New Testament idea, for in John's Gospel we read that the Holy Spirit will come to Jesus' disciples after he has departed to perpetuate his ministry in an *embodied* way,[40] that is, through the embodied agency of the disciples.[41]

SACRIFICE AND THE PRIESTHOOD OF ALL BELIEVERS

We saw earlier that another difficulty in the Reformers' deliberations concerning eucharistic sacrifice was the tension between the once-for-all nature of Christ's sacrifice on the one hand and the on going work of Christ through this sacrifice on the other. Is it possible to resolve this tension? It may be possible by considering the New Testament understanding of the priesthood of all believers. We have seen that it is possible to speak of offering Christ in the Eucharist in a derivative sense, but it might be better to speak of the church's offering being *united* with Christ's eternal offering of himself to the Father. In the church's eucharistic offering of the fruits of a redeemed world, Christians come into harmony with the life of the Triune God, being caught up, as it were, in the eternal pattern of God's acceptance of the Son's sacrifice on the cross. Of course, the central question of *why* Christians do this is fundamental to their faith: after all, what is the point? In a sense there *is* no point except for the sheer joy of coming before God in this way and being counted worthy to serve him in the world. But of course this "service" is the whole point because Christians are given the privilege and responsibility of participating in God's salvation and renewal in the world, the true and only source of which is Christ's once-for-all sacrifice on the cross. But many Christians perceive that the world is not "saved" in any final sense. Millions still suffer, experiencing poverty and pain and hunger for salvation in every sense. Calvin believed that the Eucharist is the basis for all *Christian* community, but our discussion so far has suggested that it is more than this. It is also the moment when God's "priesthood of all believers" perform their work of *being* a priestly people by representing the whole world before God and offering up prayers on its behalf.[42] And

---

40. See John 14:23 and 15:7–11.

41. At this point another important Reformed concern could be introduced into our discussion, namely the significance of the ordained priest in the Eucharist. For a discussion of Reformed ministry from a specifically URC perspective see Tucker, *Reformed Ministry*.

42. See 1 Pet 2:5. The earlier distinction between "re-presentation" and "represen-

they do not do this in a merely metaphorical or symbolic sense. But once again, there is a concern within classical Reformed theology over the ability of humanity to offer anything to God. But the point is surely that the concrete and final remedy against sin wrought through the cross of Christ is actually proclaimed and shown forth in the Eucharist and is as vividly present in this moment as can be. As such, the cross remains a *past* sanctifying event but its effects can have the same sanctifying effect in the *present* for those who have sinned and equally importantly, its present celebration can fortify the individual against *future* sin. This is not a new sacrifice or an additional one but the very same sacrifice of Calvary, brought into the church's present life experience by the power of the Holy Spirit. In the Eucharist, Christ is present in Christians who express humanity's obedience to God's loving purposes, making this ritual act a focal point for the realization of those purposes in the life of the world. Not merely a recollection, nor a re-enactment, but an entering in: a *participation* in what Christ has done and an offering that Christians make of themselves in service to the world. The Eucharist thus has the character of something on-going, providing the link between the *finished* aspect of Christ's sacrifice and the *on-going* effect of that same sacrifice, which is the continuing basis for the common life of the church and its mission to the world, a mission of self-giving and reconciling love which seeks the up-building of God's kingdom of justice and peace.

A PRACTICAL THEOLOGY OF OFFERING

The significance of "offering" in the Eucharist has been steadily developed throughout this discussion, but its significance for the daily Christian life has not yet been spelt out. In his treatment of human sin, Irenaeus sees the way to salvation in the *reconstruction* of God's creation—not through the appearance of an altogether *new* image but through the costly reclaiming of the old one "in its actual spatio-temporal and spiritual relations."[43] This leads us to the heart of what the church means when it talks about the "re-presentation" of Christ's sacrifice. The reality of the risen and ascended Lord provides the theological link between the sacrifice of Christ and the church's offering in the Eucharist. Now in

---

tation" is relevant here. In worship, the church represents the world in the sense of "standing in the place of it," such that the liturgy has a universal significance for all humanity.

43. Gunton, *The Theology of Reconciliation*, 84.

heaven and at God's right hand, Christ's life continues to be an offering on behalf of his followers, yet their own spiritual formation is bound up with a sharing in the offering of Christ, "which means also [sharing] in his painful work of recapitulation."[44] This is the church's *sanctification*, *commissioning*, and *participation* in Christ's atoning ministry. And this is a powerful insight, for the church's eucharistic offering of the first fruits of the new creation and of its members is not merely a "sign" or "witness" to their share in the reconciliation between God and humankind. Rather, by participating in the eucharistic liturgy, Christians show that the reconciliation wrought by God in Christ is actually having a visible effect on real human relationships in the church. When people hungry for such reconciliation and healing see that it is real, and what it rests on, then Christ can be said to be working and speaking through the church, helping the world to overcome its unbelief. The world may then in turn be led to give praise to the Father in heaven.[45] Here one perhaps begins to see the opportunity for rich meaning in the United Reformed Church's affirmation that, "in obedience to the Lord's command his people *show forth his sacrifice* on the cross." And this is an understanding that has profound dimensions for a Reformed understanding of the "priesthood of all believers," because it embraces the richness of resources brought to God by worshippers in the Eucharist. Through the offering of their *bodies*, by their physical presence at the eucharistic liturgy, Christians become offerings of the new creation, receiving the gift of their own sanctified lives back in the sacrament in order to be sent out once again to be representatives of Christ in the world.

In all these ways we may speak of "eucharistic sacrifice" in a Reformed service. And this is not to say anything completely new, for as we have seen, the Reformed tradition affirms the sacrificial character of the Eucharist. The Reformers did not seek to eliminate the idea of sacrifice in the Eucharist but to purify it. Inevitably, however, their purging of the liturgy made sacrifice an invisible reality. All gestures and symbolism that may have given the impression of a sacrifice independent of the sacrifice of the cross being offered on the altar were abolished. But has the time come for the United Reformed Church to review its practice as a member of the Reformed Christian tradition? Recent studies of lit-

---

44. Ibid., 89.
45. See Matt. 5:16.

urgy have confirmed that good liturgy grounds right belief.[46] Therefore it is very important that appropriate words are used, but what about the importance of ritual, symbol, and gesture? It has often been said that actions speak louder than words. Perhaps this is especially true of the church's encounter with God in the Eucharist. A significant insight from recent discussions is that liturgy is a particular medium; it is what it is when *performed* or *enacted*. In other words, it requires the physicality of participants.[47] From a purely individual standpoint, liturgy requires *bodily* presence and requires ritual that enables people to act together to affirm a common identity. This is highly significant for the symbolism of eucharistic sacrifice in that Christians offer themselves as *one body*, a priestly community. In light of these insights, one can identify several common practices in the eucharistic worship of many United Reformed Church congregations that are symbolically significant and worthy of comment. In the latest worship liturgy from the United Reformed Church, the "First Order of Holy Communion" begins with words of invitation taken from the Scriptures followed by the offertory. The suggested instruction is that the gifts of bread and wine may be brought to the table at this point, along with the collection plates.[48] This seems to be a most appropriate liturgical gesture at this point of the service, given all that has been discussed concerning the legitimacy of the church's offering in the Eucharist. However, this could be included as a permanent and essential act before the eucharistic prayer rather than an optional one. The other common practice in many United Reformed Church congregations is to receive individual pieces of bread and individual cups of wine where they are seated. This, however, seems to be a most unfortunate practice in terms of liturgical participation, failing to take seriously both the response of the faithful to the president's invitation and the words used after the offertory, "Brothers and sisters, by the mercies of God present your bodies as a living sacrifice, holy and acceptable to God."[49] The Eucharist is the means through which God challenges the church's memories of personal and collective sin, inviting repentance and offering assurance of God's pardon, then truly unites those gathered as one body to share one bread. This cannot help but be a concrete

46. Jones et al., *The Study of the Liturgy*, 6.

47. Ibid., 52–8.

48. *Worship: from The United Reformed Church*, 7.

49. Ibid.

channel of God's grace, around which the congregation expresses its unity and upon which each member is utterly dependent; a reality that is surely better expressed by people coming forward to receive the bread and wine.

CONCLUSION

The Eucharist clearly has a sacrificial element. But as we have seen, the history of how these words should be interpreted in language and symbolism has been controversial. The overall conclusion of this discussion is that the language and symbolism of eucharistic sacrifice must have a vital and meaningful place in a Christian service of Word and sacrament. This is especially true of the Reformed tradition, which places such an emphasis on the priesthood of all believers. This study has shown how there is a way to conceive of the Christian community *offering* Christ in the Eucharist in a way that does not compromise the sufficiency and finality of the cross. One that takes seriously the covenant relationship the church has with God and the responsibility Christians are given to serve God in the world and to pray on behalf of it, as the benefits of Christ's once-for-all sacrifice are continually shown forth as a living memory and offered to the world today. This, in turn, may enrich the church's worship and ground its missionary work for peace and justice in a vital and life-giving encounter with God.

9

Why Should I Sing the Psalms?

The Reformed Tradition of Psalmody[1]

BY BARBARA DOUGLAS

MY NAME IS BARBARA Douglas. I'm originally from Iowa, I'm married to Nigel, a minister in the United Reformed Church, and we have six children. More to the point, I was brought up in the Dutch Reformed tradition, trained as a musician at the University of Iowa, studied the aesthetics of music at the Institute for Christian Studies in Toronto, and helped to catalogue the Elias Library of Hymnology at Westminster College in Cambridge. I've experienced worship in many places and traditions, and I've always been struck by the richness and variety of musical expression. Everything from Gregorian chant to hard rock, from classical to folk, jazz to rap: any kind of music imaginable can be and is being used in praise of God! Praise God that this is so! And yet the worldwide Reformed tradition has a distinct contribution to make to all this, one that I believe deserves attention. In this essay I will examine a little more closely what Calvin and the translators and musicians who worked with him achieved. Then I will outline how this tradition has been handed down, re-interpreted and used in Reformed churches around the world since then. Finally I suggest some ways this tradition

---

1. This essay is an adapted version of a participative talk on psalm-singing, held in the chapel of Westminster College, Cambridge on an evening during the conference. Participants sang the psalm-settings that Barbara cites in the text (though, not all the verses of the longer psalms). The editors have attempted to retain something of the informal nature of this event in the adapted text.

may be used now. I will provide selected musical examples throughout, including some different versions of Psalm 42 as a point of comparison. The first example I cite is perhaps the best-known musical offering from Calvin's Geneva: Psalm 134 (Old Hundredth).

Genevan 134 (Old Hundredth)

Louis Bourgeois, 1551

You servants of the Lord our God
who work and pray both day and night,
in God's own house lift up your hands
and praise the Lord with all your might.

The Lord God bless you from his throne,
the Lord show you his gracious face.
He who created heaven and earth
give you his everlasting peace.[2]

THE EMPHASIS ON CONGREGATIONAL SINGING
IN THE PROTESTANT REFORMATION

The Reformed tradition of music in worship can be summed up in two words—metrical psalms. "Metrical" means verse translations of the psalms, with a strophic structure, i.e. broken up into verses in which each line has a regular number of syllables, so each verse fits the same tune. "Psalms" means all of all 150 poems from the Book of Psalms, along with a few select canticles from the Bible. Many, many traditions sing metrical songs of praise, hymns especially. All Christians draw from the book of Psalms to some extent. It was John Calvin's insistence on restricting public worship music to vernacular metrical psalms that provided the impetus for what became distinctively Reformed. Calvin

2. Translation and versification of Psalm 134 by Calvin Seerveld, *Psalter Hymnal* (1987), 134. Used by permission © Calvin Seerveld.

rejected the chanting of psalms and liturgy in Latin, the practice of the medieval church, in favor of quasi-popular tunes the congregation could use to sing the psalms in their own language; and unlike Martin Luther, he restricted the lyrics to psalms and other biblical texts. The glory of late medieval and renaissance choral music in worship was no match for the hunger for the Bible that was revealed as the Word was translated into the vernacular. The Protestant reformers wanted all the people to understand everything that happened in worship and to participate as fully as possible. This desire was worked-out differently by different leaders. In Germany, Luther kept everything of the old forms that he could, including some plainchant and even some Latin where people could be expected to understand it. He did not ban the use of choirs, though he also encouraged everyone to sing the hymns (called "chorales") that he wrote and collected. Most often the early Lutherans used familiar tunes with new texts. For Luther, congregational singing was an extension of preaching and teaching, so he did not restrict his texts to what was biblical, but included lots of doctrine as well. People took to this kind of singing in worship readily wherever the Reformation took hold, partly because hymn singing had been a popular part of domestic piety since the late Middle Ages, and one of the first signs of the Reformation was the singing of psalm translations to popular tunes. In England, the language of worship was changed from Latin to English whenever the reformers had the political upper hand. There was some effort to encourage the singing of simplified chants in English by congregations, but choirs retained their supremacy, and the matter was left to each individual parish. This led to a wonderful flowering of choral music in English for use in worship by choirs, but congregations often tended to lapse into silence. In Switzerland, Zwingli represented the opposite tendency to both Luther and the English—he abolished music from worship altogether. Calvin seems initially to have agreed with Zwingli, but through the influence of Bucer, and from pastoral experience, he came to view congregational singing as invaluable, not as an aid to preaching, but as an aid to prayer. The Geneva Psalter was the direct result of Calvin's reflections on the pastoral and theological meaning of music. He had had the usual instruction in medieval and classical theories about music, and he also observed early Lutheran and Reformed congregational singing. Although he wrote that music was unnecessary for private prayer before he had pastoral charge of a congregation; by

1537 he listed music as one of three things necessary for congregational life and public worship to be rightly ordered.[3] He always considered music in the context of prayer rather than teaching. Singing together is, for him, a form of praying together. The logical outcome of this was the thought that private singing is also prayer, so that he eventually wanted all secular songs to be replaced by sung psalms, so that people might pray without ceasing as Paul commanded (we may conclude from this that people sang habitually in daily life!)

CALVIN ON THE POWER OF SINGING

Calvin believed that "song has great force and vigor to arouse and inflame hearts" for good or for ill.[4] Music must therefore have a text, to which it must be subservient. Only Scripture is good enough for the praise of God and wholly without evil. Calvin wrote that a text set to music "pierces the heart that much more strongly and enters into it; just as through a funnel wine is poured into a container, so also venom and corruption are distilled to the depth of the heart by the melody"[5] if the text is unholy. So, when the people's prayers are "so cold that we should be greatly ashamed and confused,"[6] they must sing the psalms, and be encouraged through them to pray more ardently. "The psalms can stimulate us to raise our hearts to God and arouse us to an ardor in invoking as well as in exalting with praises the glory of [God's] name. Moreover, by this one will recognize of what advantage and consolation the Pope and his creatures have deprived the church, for he has distorted the psalms, which should be true spiritual songs, into a murmuring among themselves without any understanding."[7] It is vital that congregations pray with understanding, in their own language, and the music for the psalms must fit the context of prayer—"There must always be concern that the song be neither light nor frivolous, but have gravity and majesty."[8] They should also be learned from memory, "After the intelligence must follow the heart and the affection which is impossible

3. Garside, "The Origins of Calvin's Theology of Music," 10.
4. Ibid., 32.
5. Ibid.
6. Ibid., 10.
7. Ibid.
8. Ibid., 18.

unless we have the hymn imprinted on our memory in order never to cease from singing."[9] Calvin's statement that music should have "gravity and majesty" can raise hackles today. We more often worry that music for worship must be lively. But Calvin never said music should be dull: he approved the music of the Genevan Psalter, which, while never frivolous, is often lively. Visitors to Strasbourg and Geneva commented in letters home how enthusiastic the singing was. In Geneva, and wherever that example was followed, metrical psalm singing ensured the participation of all worshippers in public prayer, and incidentally provided a way to teach Scripture to the illiterate: since most psalms were assigned a "proper" tune[10] in the psalter, the music could aid in the memorization and recall of the psalms. In Geneva, Calvin commissioned translations and music for the psalter. By 1562 the work was complete. The musicians who worked on the psalter, most notably Louis Bourgeois, did a remarkable job of using the richness of sixteenth century musical language to match the meaning of each psalm, yielding a wide variety of expression. We have already sung the best-known example. It is known in English as "Old Hundredth," but it was written for Psalm 134.[11] Everything about it justifies its popularity. It is simple, economical, and yet grand, in a major key with a regular rhythm.

The next example I would like to look at is Psalm 42.[12] Here the tune is memorable and lilting, with gentle dance rhythms that suits the water imagery without negating the many changes of mood from yearning to sorrow to vindication and hope. The psalm is a long one, especially if it is joined to Psalm 43 which shares the same repeated refrain, but the tune moves along with a spring (assuming it is taken at a reasonably quick pace and that the original rhythm is retained) that wards off the feeling that one sometimes has of a hymn that will never end.

9. Ibid., 33.

10. That is to say, a tune shared by no other text.

11. *Psalter Hymnal* (1987), 134.

12. Ibid., 42.

Genevan 42

Louis Bourgeois, 1551

As a deer in want of water, so I long for you, O Lord.
All my heart and being falter, thirsting for your living word.
When shall I behold your face? When shall I receive your grace?
When shall I, your praises voicing, come before you with rejoicing?

Bitter tears of lamentation are my food by night and day.
In my deep humiliation "Where is now your God?" they say.
When my sorrows weigh on me, then I bring to memory
how with throngs I would assemble, shouting praises in your
    temple.

O my soul, why are you grieving, why disquieted in me?
Put your hope in God, believing he will still your refuge be.
I again shall praise his grace for the comfort of his face;
he will show his help and favor for he is my God and Savior.

From the land beyond the Jordan, in my grief I think of you;
from the foothills of Mount Hermon I will still remember you.
As the waters plunge and leap, stormy troubles o'er me sweep.
Day and night God's song is with me as a prayer to him
    who loves me.

I will say to God, my fortress "Why have you forgotten me?
Why must I proceed in sadness, hounded by the enemy?"
Their rebukes and scoffing words pierce my bones like pointed
    swords,
as they say with proud defiance, "Where is God, your firm
    reliance?"

O my soul, why are you grieving, why disquieted in me?
Put your hope in God, believing he will still your refuge be.

I again shall praise his grace for the comfort of his face;
he will show his help and favor for he is my God and Savior.

Vindicate me, God, my Father, come and plead my urgent cause,
for my enemies forever threaten me and flout your laws.
I am safe with you alone; why do you reject your own?
Lord, I need your help and blessing; keep me safe from this
    oppressing.

Send your light and truth to lead me; send them forth to be
    my guide.
To your mountain let them bring me, to the place where
    you reside.
Then O God, I will come near and before your throne appear,
to my Savior praises bringing with the harp and joyful singing.

O my soul, why are you grieving, why disquieted in me?
Put your hope in God, believing he will still your refuge be.
I again shall praise his grace for the comfort of his face;
he will show his help and favor for he is my God and Savior.[13]

One of the most notable things about the psalms is how dark the palette can be, and the Geneva tunes do not avoid this. Let's consider Psalm 51. Notable among its many choral settings is Allegri's "Miserere," with its soaring, piercing soprano line. Geneva 51 is equally haunting, while being much easier to sing. It is minor, with an irregular rhythm in an unusual meter. It is a long tune for a long psalm, a common feature among these tunes which helps avoid the ennui of endless repetitions of a too-short tune paired with a long text.

13. Psalm 42–3; versification *Psalter Hymnal* (1987) © CRC Publications, used by permission of Faith Alive Resources.

Genevan 51

Louis Bourgeois, harm. Goudimel

Be merciful, be merciful, O God.
According to your steadfast love, have mercy.
blot out my sin in your abundant mercy.
wash all my sin away and make me clean.

I know my sin, it will not leave my mind.
Against you, only you, I have been sinning.
So you are just in judging what I did.
Even before my birth my life was tainted.

You want me truthful in my inmost heart;
you teach me in my secret heart your wisdom.
To wash me clean again, purge me with hyssop
and make me whiter than new-fallen snow.

Fill me with joy and gladness, make me sing,
and let the bones you broke begin their dancing.
O hide your face from sins that cause me shame.
Blot out the stain of all my foul transgressions.

Create in me, O God, a new, clean heart
and make my spirit pure and right within me.
O do not cast me helpless from your presence.
Your Holy Spirit must not go from me.

Restore to me the joy of being yours.
Uphold me with a free and willing spirit.
Then I will teach transgressors of your ways.
Then sinners will return again to serve you.

Deliver me from guilt of blood, O God.
O God, you are the God of my salvation.
My tongue will sing then that I am delivered.
Open my lips, O Lord, to sing your praise.

For you take no delight in sacrifice.
You take no pleasure in the gifts I offer.
A broken spirit is acceptable.
You will not scorn a heart contrite and broken.

Be good to Zion; Lord, in mercy hear.
The walls around Jerusalem lie broken.
Rebuild the walls, Lord: help us to rebuild them.
Be good to Zion; Lord in mercy hear.

Then you will take delight in us again,
in gifts we bring to lay upon your altar.
Then you will take delight in us again,
in proper sacrifice and righteous service.[14]

Now as a complete contrast, let's turn to Psalm 47. Here the major tune has jaunty, rejoicing dance rhythms with strong syncopation, which are altogether appropriate for the words.

---

14. *Psalter Hymnal* (1987), 51, versification by Stanley Wiersma, 1980. © CRC Publications, used by permission of Faith Alive Christian Resources.

Genevan 47 (harmonised)

Louis Bourgeois, harm. Goudimel

Nations, clap your hands; shout with joy, you lands!
Awesome is the Lord; spread his fame abroad.
He rules every land with a mighty hand.
God brings nations low, he subdues each foe.
From his mighty throne God protects his own.
Our inheritance is our sure defense.

God goes up on high with a joyful cry.
with a mighty shout; people, sing it out!
Let your voices bring praises to our King.
Praise him with a song; praise with heart and tongue;
praise with every skill; praise with mind and will.
God rules all the earth; magnify his worth.

God reigns over all rulers great and small.
Leaders of the world, servants of the Lord,
rally round his throne; he is God alone.
Sing before him now, in his presence bow.
God of Abraham! God of every land!
Worship and adore God forevermore.[15]

15. *Psalter Hymnal* (1987), 47. Text: versification *Psalter Hymnal*, 1987. © CRC
Publications. Tune: Louis Bourgeios, 1551; Harmony: Claude Goudimel, 1564. Used by
permission of Faith Alive Christian Resources.

In Geneva all these psalms, in their new translations and settings, were gradually taught to the congregations. "For a beginning the little children are to be taught; then with time all the church will be able to follow," wrote Calvin.[16] And I can recommend from experience that if you want to introduce something new, getting the children to do it for the people first will avoid a great deal of grumbling! For public worship they sang in unison, without accompaniment, but evidently very enthusiastically, and (reading between the lines of eyewitness accounts) probably not slowly. Very soon four part harmonizations appeared for use at home. The Geneva Psalter became very popular, and very closely associated with Calvinist worship. In many places it was adopted directly (in France), or, as in Holland, translations were made which fit the Genevan tunes. I even have a copy in Hungarian. So one of the biggest elements of the Reformed tradition worldwide is actually the Geneva Psalter itself, still actively used today in many places.

The years took their toll on the psalter, however. Unaccompanied singing, in a tradition that tended to emphasize solemnity over enthusiasm, led to slower and slower tempi and a loss of rhythmic shape over time, so today the "Geneva Jigs" that Queen Elizabeth I complained about have the reputation of being dirges. Even the printing of the Geneva tunes reflects this. The first time I encountered Genevan 42, it had been made "isorhythmic"—that is, all the syncopation of the original rhythm had been removed.[17] This is still a lovely tune, and appears in similar guises in many places, including the Scottish Psalter, but it has lost all the jauntiness of its original rhythm, and is, I think, much less interesting.

16. Garside, op. cit., 16.
17. *Psalter Hymnal* (1957), 74.

Genevan 42 (isorhythmic)

Louis Bourgeois

PSALM SINGING IN THE BRITISH ISLES

In the British Isles, the reception of metrical psalmody was a bit different. Where clergy were enthusiastic about Calvin's teaching (most notably in Scotland), metrical psalmody was introduced, but at the time all popular songs, and the lyrics for them, used just a few meters, mostly Common Meter (8686) and Long Meter (8888). Only a few of the Geneva tunes fit these parameters, so when Scottish and English reformers made metrical translations of the psalms they wrote or adopted tunes of their own, all in the same few meters, rather than adopt the Genevan tunes. Hence, in Scotland and England, the tunes were more or less interchangeable. Without the strong link between particular words and particular tunes, both were harder to remember. Scottish Psalters developed the charming peculiarity of split pages, with the tunes on the top section and the words on the bottom, so that one can put almost any Psalm with almost any tune. As an example, one can sing the Scottish versification of Psalm 42 to tune number 61, "Dundee" or "French" in the Scottish Psalter of 1929.[18] This is a very typical Scottish psalter translation and tune: very regular rhythm, major key. The translation may be a little bit labored, but the whole psalm is there, as it was in the Geneva Psalter.

---

18. Tune "Dundee/French," words beginning "Like as the hart for water-brooks/ in thirst doth pant and bray."

Dundee/French (Scottish Psalter 1615)

Scottish Psalter 1615

Like as the hart for water-brooks
in thirst doth pant and bray;
So pants my longing soul, O God,
that come to thee I may.

My soul for God, the living God,
doth thirst: when shall I near
unto thy countenance approach,
and in God's sight appear?

My tears have unto me been meat,
both in the night and day,
while unto me continually
"Where is thy God?" they say.

My soul is pourèd out in me,
when this I think upon;
because that with the multitude
I heretofore had gone:

With them into God's house I went,
with voice of joy and praise;
yea, with the multitude that kept
the solemn holy days.

O why art thou cast down, my soul?
Why in me so dismay'd?
Trust God, for I shall praise him yet,
his count'nance is mine aid.

My God, my soul's cast down in me;
thee therefore mind I will
from Jordan's land, the Hermonites,
and ev'n from Mizar hill.

At the noise of thy water-spouts
deep unto deep doth call;
thy breaking waves pass over me,
yea, and thy billows all.

His loving-kindness yet the Lord
command will in the day,
his song's with me by night; to God,
by whom I live, I'll pray:

And I will say to God my rock,
"Why me forgett'st thou so?
Why, for my foes' oppression,
thus mourning do I go?"

'Tis as a sword within my bones,
when my foes me upbraid;
Ev'n when by them, Where is thy God?
'tis daily to me said.

O why art thou cast down, my soul?
Why, thus with grief opprest?
Art thou disquieted in me?
In God still hope and rest:

For yet I know I shall him praise,
who graciously to me
The health is of my countenance,
yea, mine own God is he.[19]

For many years in Scotland there was little or no professional musical input in most congregations. A cantor led the singing by means of "lining out" the opening phrase, the congregation immediately followed the cantor's lead. Most people had neither the words nor the music in front of them, so the tunes had to be simple and memorable. Many tunes did not survive. At one point in the seventeenth century the psalter was published with only 12 common tunes. Gradually new tunes were added which stuck, in new musical styles as they evolved. Some pairings, of course, became classics like the nineteenth-century tune *Crimond* with Psalm 23.

19. *Scottish Psalter*, No. 42.

Crimond

Jessie Seymour Irvine, 1872

The Lord's my Shepherd, I'll not want:
he makes me down to lie
in pastures green; he leadeth me
the quiet waters by.

My soul he doth restore again,
and me to walk doth make
within the paths of righteousness,
ev'n for his own name's sake.

Yea, though I walk through death's dark vale,
yet will I fear no ill;
for thou art with me, and thy rod
and staff me comfort still.

My table thou hast furnishèd,
in presence of my foes;
my head thou dost with oil anoint,
and my cup overflows.

Goodness and mercy all my life
shall surely follow me;
and in God's house for evermore
my dwelling-place shall be.[20]

As with the Genevan tunes, over time unaccompanied singing resulted in slower and slower tempi. It also resulted in a quite unique tradition of improvised elaboration on the tunes, a tradition that still exists in some remoter places. In England, as I alluded to earlier, the triumph of Calvinism was much less complete, and the chanting of psalms by choirs has continued to the present day, though now of course in English rather than in Latin. Metrical psalms were used as well, and gained prominence in times and places where Reformed thinking dominated, most notably among the Puritans, and later the Dissenting churches. Many collections were published, notable among them those of Sternhold and Hopkins,[21] and a little later Tate and Brady. Strictly speaking, many of these latter were paraphrases rather than translations, and tunes were published separately, collected from many sources. "Martyrdom" by Hugh Wilson (1766–1824) is a tune that is frequently used for Tate and Brady's paraphrase of Psalm 42.

20. *Scottish Psalter*, No. 23.

21. *The Whole Book of Psalms, collected into English Metre*, 1562, published by John Day.

Martyrdom

Hugh Wilson (1766-1824)
adpt. R. A. Smith (1780-1829)

As pants the hart for cooling streams,
when heated in the chase,
so longs my soul, O God, for thee,
and thy refreshing grace.

For thee, my God, the living God,
my thirsty soul doth pine;
O when shall I behold thy face,
thou Majesty divine?

Tears are my constant food, while thus
insulting foes upbraid,
"Deluded wretch, where's now thy God?
and where his promis'd aid?"

I sigh when-e'er my musing thoughts
those happy days present,
When I with troops of pious friends
thy temple did frequent.

When I advanc'd with songs of praise,
my solemn vows to pay,
And led the joyful sacred throng
that kept the festal day.

Why restless, why cast down my soul?
Trust God, and he'll employ
his aid for thee, and change these sighs
to thankful hymns of joy.

My soul's cast down, O God, but thinks
on thee and Sion still;
From Jordan's Bank from Hermon's Heights,
and Missar's humbler Hill.

One trouble calls another on,
and bursting o'er my head,
Fall spouting down, till round my soul
a roaring sea is spread.

But when thy presence, Lord of life,
has once dispell'd this storm,
To thee I'll midnight anthems sing,
and all my vows perform.

God of my strength, how long shall I,
like one forgotten, mourn—
forlorn, forsaken, and exposed
to my oppressor's scorn?

My heart is pierced, as with a sword,
while thus my foes upbraid:
"Vain boaster, where is now thy God?
And where his promised aid?"

Why restless, why cast down, my soul?
Hope still, and thou shalt sing
the praise of him who is thy God,
thy health's eternal spring. [22]

Hymn singing began to supplement, and eventually to supplant, psalm singing in the eighteenth century. The trend gained impetus from the popularity of Isaac Watts' work, although hymns had been used in private and domestic devotions since the Middle Ages. Isaac Watts began by making metrical translations of the psalms, but he felt that they

22. Tate and Brady, *A New Version of the Psalms of David*, 1696, 1754, Psalm 42.

needed to be amended to reflect specifically Christian doctrines, so he published "Christianized" paraphrases of the psalms, and then moved on to entirely new hymns. A good example of one of his paraphrases is Psalm 136, to the tune "Duke Street" from Boyd's *Psalm & Hymn Tunes*, 1793.[23] In England, hymns that were not necessarily related to psalms became widely accepted in public worship in the nineteenth century.

Duke Street

John Hatton, 1793

Give to our God immortal praise,
mercy and truth are all his ways:
wonders of grace to God belong,
repeat his mercies in your song.

Give to the Lord of lords renown;
the King of kings with glory crown:
his mercies ever shall endure,

23. Words by Isaac Watts, *Psalms of David Imitated in the Language of the New Testament*, 1719, (tune by John Hatton) which appeared in Boyd's *Select Collection of Psalm and Hymn Tunes*, 1793. The two became associated with each other in the *Congregational Hymnary* of 1916, according to *Companion to Congregational Praise*.

when lords and kings are known no more.

He built the earth, he spread the sky,
and fixed the starry lights on high,
wonders of grace to God belong,
repeat his mercies in your song.

He fills the sun with morning light,
he bids the moon direct the night:
his mercies ever shall endure
when suns and moons shall shine no more.

He sent his Son with power to save
from guilt and darkness and the grave:
wonders of grace to God belong,
repeat his mercies in your song.

Through this vain world he guides our feet,
and leads us to his mercy-seat;
his mercies ever shall endure,
when this vain world shall be no more.[24]

These, then, are the main strands of Reformed psalm-singing down
the years: the continued use of the Geneva Psalter on the European
continent and wherever those traditions were transplanted; the distinctive feel and practice of the evolving Scottish Psalter with its own
conservative cantor-led tradition of lining-out; and English (and also
American) metrical psalms and paraphrases of psalms still jostling for
place among the proliferation of hymns. Just as in recent years hymn
writing and music for worship generally has seen an explosion of new
material and inter-denominational cross-fertilization, so psalm singing
is being rediscovered and explored in new ways in many places. Most
of the examples I have cited are from hymnals and psalters that are in
current use. The Geneva tunes, particularly, have in many places been
rediscovered as "jigs"—full of life and vitality if sung with their original
rhythms. The Christian Reformed Church's *Psalter Hymnal* has set new
metrical English translations to about 40 of these in the 1987 edition, far
more than were in the previous (1957) edition, and all in their original
rhythms. The 1987 book is also notable for insisting on complete texts
of the psalms, even 119, which runs to 22 stanzas! They have made finding the psalms to sing easy too: numbers 1–150 in the *Psalter Hymnal*

---

24. *Rejoice and Sing*, 94.

all correspond to the original Book of Psalms numbering. These are all metrical psalm settings, though there are others among the hymns further on. Another hymnal that has made a feature of the psalms is *Praise*, published in 2000 by a group associated with the Fellowship of Independent Evangelical churches. Although it is not consciously trying to be Reformed as such, it contains examples from all the strands we've looked at, along with many new translations. Not all the psalms are present in full, but the editors have tried to be fairly complete: Psalm 119 is represented by 7 tunes setting successive sections of the psalm. Timothy Dudley-Smith has 53 psalms and hymns in this book, including 19 metrical psalms. Here too the first 150 items correspond to the 150 psalms. A glance through the Scriptural index of any new worship songbook will reveal a number of psalm-settings and many more songs inspired by psalms. Springing immediately to mind are, "As the Deer" by Martin Nystrom,[25] and "The Lord's My Shepherd" by Stuart Townend.[26] Many, many other examples could be cited, I am sure.

WHY SING THE PSALMS?

I have not yet really offered a defense of the tradition of psalm singing, as opposed to hymn singing, or of metrical versus chanted settings. I will leave you with a few thoughts on that topic. Singing the psalms in their entirety can widen our emotional and spiritual horizons—the psalmist is never afraid to be honest, or to confront pain and anger. The psalms let us, as Calvin wrote, sing our prayers of fear and despair and guilt as well as of praise. I sang a hymn in church inspired by Geneva 51 on the Sunday after the attacks of 9/11, for instance.[27] The choice of metrical psalmody or chanting in one form or another is, perhaps, more a matter of what any given congregation is going to find conducive to worship. Most of the churches I have been in have found metrical forms more natural, but I have been in congregations that chanted quite happily. The key, I feel, is the principle of maximum congregational participation, with as much biblical material as possible. Calvin knew what he was doing.

---

25. © 1983, Martin Nystrom/Restoration Music, administered by Sovereign Music UK.

26. © 1996 Kingsway's Thankyou Music.

27. "A Congregational Lament", 576 in the *Psalter Hymnal* (1987) to the tune Genevan 51 with words by Calvin Seerveld beginning "Why, Lord, must evil seem to get its way?"

10

A Sermon[1]

Isaiah 6:1–8; Revelation 4:1–11; John 4:7–26

by Colin Thompson

L ET ME REMIND YOU of some of the scriptural places we have visited and the things that we have heard there. We have stood in the
Temple and listened to Solomon's dedication prayer, with its awareness
of the contradiction between constructing sacred space and a God who
can never be confined by human structures, whether in stone or paint or
words. We have heard Amos warning that ritual divorced from justice
is abhorrent to God. We have argued about the words we use in worship, about venerable words, which have come to us down the centuries
and which attempt to express the dynamic nature of the Godhead, and
about other words and images which shed a different scriptural light, especially when such traditions become problematic—a process all forms
of reformation and renewal must face. Now, in this Eucharist, we have
come back to the Temple and watched with Isaiah as its architecture
comes alive, the carved seraphim fly amid the clouds of incense and the
foundations of the house are shaken. We have witnessed his unexpected
encounter with the divine presence; we have heard his shame, a man of
unclean lips, and not only his but that of the whole people, a nation of
unclean lips. In the midst of his sense of complete inadequacy he hears
the voice which asks who shall be sent; his lips are cleansed, his words

1. First preached in the chapel of Westminster College, Cambridge, on 6 September
2007, during the final Eucharist at the *Reforming Worship* conference.

are renewed, and he can respond, "Here am I. Send me." The pattern is set before us: when worship comes alive we know our smallness and our shame; yet that is when God's fire has power to refine and cleanse, and that in turn is when paralysis gives way to movement and mission. I wonder if you have noticed how in the most recent liturgies of the United Reformed Church the words of forgiveness are therefore followed by the call to follow Christ: Take up your cross; follow me.

We have entered into the heavenly Temple with the writer of Hebrews, through language dense will allusion to the ritual law of the Hebrew Scriptures and have followed a typological progression from foreshadowing to fulfillment, from repeated human attempts to placate an offended God to the sacrifice offered once for all for the sins of the world. We have reflected on this sacrament and on the place of the language of offering and sacrifice in Reformed theology and liturgy, historically contentious but rich in meaning. Now, in this Eucharist, we stand on the threshold of the worship of the heavenly Temple, described in a language of poetry and symbol, which is the only language we have for things unseen. Our worship is the moment when for a brief moment earth and heaven are joined, and our prayers and the prayers of the saints are united, our poor earthbound words struggling to catch the echo of their praises in the presence of the Holy One.

We have heard how immediately after the wilderness temptations of Jesus, Luke takes us to his first sermon, in the synagogue at Capernaum, small and humble in comparison with the splendors of the Temple, reminding us that the preaching ministry of Jesus could only begin after he had passed through the most testing of experiences. We have been with Paul as he wrestled with the tension between freedom of the gifts of the Spirit and the need for order, understanding, and interpretation. We have thought about the world of work and about communication, especially in the preaching of the word in contemporary culture. And now, in this Eucharist, we have stood with Jesus on a hot afternoon by a well, as he exchanged humorous and good-natured banter with a Samaritan woman not so much about her interesting private life as about the nature of God and the need worship itself to be God-centered and Spirit-filled.

That is some of the journey we have been sharing. There has been much more, not least through the riches of music. We have been consciously Reformed, because that is our tradition; but we have not neglected what my role model Father Jack[2] learnt with some difficulty to call "an ecumenical matter," because we do not believe the church began at the Reformation: we are catholic Christians who have inherited the treasures and the tensions of the first fourteen Christian centuries, and who grieve that thereafter we have grown apart. Or perhaps the treasures are the tensions: the creative space between language which imagines God and language which is wholly inadequate to do more than stammer; between a sense of our own limitations and unworthiness and the call of God which takes us as we are; between the earthbound and the heavenly; between freedom and order; between the culture of our age and the principles of theology; between our particular traditions and the one holy catholic and apostolic church through the ages and in the new Jerusalem. If we can accept such tensions as gifts to be shared rather than possessions to be defended, and if we can explore the terrain they offer, in humility and with a listening ear, doors will open, paths will be smoothed, and our worship will lead us to grow, however imperceptibly, towards the fullness of the stature of Christ: to whom be glory in the Church, now and always. Amen.

2. Fr Jack is a character in the situation comedy *Father Ted*, produced by Hat Trick Productions for British broadcaster Channel 4, 1995–98.

11

Evening and Morning Liturgies

Orders for Evening Prayer, Morning Prayer, and the Lord's Supper[1]

BY COLIN THOMPSON

EVENING PRAYER FOR MONDAY

Liturgy taken from John Hunter, Devotional Services for Public Worship, 1903—Eighth Order.[2]

SCRIPTURE SENTENCES

The sentences end with . . .
I will hear what God the Lord will speak; for he will speak peace unto his people and to his saints.
Speak, Lord, and let thy servants hear.
All kneeling or bowing

PRAYER OF INVOCATION

---

1. The following are the liturgies that Colin Thompson, Chaplain to the conference, used to lead the conference in worship. The numbers refer to hymns, chants, psalms, or prayers in the United Reformed Church hymn book *Rejoice and Sing*. As is the convention, words in bold are spoken by all.

2. 7th Edition, Glasgow: James MacElhose and Sons, 1903. Reprint, Whitefish: Kessinger, 2010.

PRAYER OF CONFESSION

> Let us humbly confess our sins to Almighty God.
> **Almighty Father, Lord of heaven and earth,**
> **we confess that we have sinned against thee**
> **in thought, word and deed.**
> **Have mercy upon us, O Lord;**
> **have mercy upon us, after thy great goodness;**
> **according to the multitude of thy mercies**
> **put away our offences, and cleanse us from our sins;**
> **and teach us to love what is right and to do it forever. Amen.**

PRAYER

PSALM

> Psalm 122—563 in *Rejoice and Sing*, "How pleased and blest was I"

LESSON

> 1 Kings 8:22–30
> *All standing*
> Jesus said: The first of all the commandments is,
> Hear, O Israel, the Lord thy God is one Lord;
> and thou shalt love the Lord thy God with all thy heart,
> and with all thy soul, and with all thy mind, and with all thy
>   strength.
> This is the first and great commandment.
> **Lord, have mercy upon us,**
> **and incline our hearts to keep this law.**
> And the second is like, namely this,
> Thou shalt love thy neighbor as thyself.
> **Lord, have mercy upon us,**
> **and incline our hearts to keep this law.**
> Lift up your hearts.
> **We will lift them up unto the Lord.**
> At all times and in all places we will give thanks unto thee,
> O Lord, Holy Father, Almighty, Everlasting God.
> Therefore with angels and archangels,
> and with all the company of heaven,
> we laud and magnify thy glorious Name,

evermore praising thee and saying:
Holy, holy, holy, Lord God of Hosts;
heaven and earth are full of thy glory. Amen.

A PRAYER OF INTERCESSION

Response:
We beseech thee to hear us, O God.
(ending . . .) God be merciful unto us sinners:
Amen.
Our Father, who art in heaven . . .

HYMN

527 in *Rejoice and Sing*, "Jesus, our mighty Lord"

PRAYER AND BENEDICTION

MORNING PRAYER FOR TUESDAY AND WEDNESDAY

Liturgy from Worship: from the United Reformed Church, 2003[3]

Our Father in heaven
Let us wait upon the Lord, God of heaven and earth.
Let us worship God in spirit and in truth.

SCRIPTURE SENTENCE

Hallowed be your Name
O Lord open our lips:
and our mouth shall proclaim your praise.
Give thanks to the Lord of lords:
for his steadfast love endures forever.

PSALM

Tuesday—Psalm 145—732 in *Rejoice and Sing*
Wednesday—Psalm 84—703 in *Rejoice and Sing*

Glory to the Father and to the Son
and to the Holy Spirit

---

3. London: © The United Reformed Church, UK, 2003.

as it was in the beginning is now
and shall be forever. Amen.
Your kingdom come, your will be done, on earth as in heaven

Prayer for God's kingdom

After each prayer . . .
Your kingdom come:
your will be done.
Give us today our daily bread
Lord, break the bread of your word among us:
and nourish us with your truth.

Scripture Reading

Tuesday—Luke 4:1–21
Wednesday—Amos 5:14–15, 21–24

Forgive us our sins as we forgive those who sin against us
Let us confess our sins to God
and resolve to accept and share his forgiveness.
Silence
Lord God most merciful,
we confess that we have sinned,
through our own fault,
and in common with others,
in thought, word and deed,
and through what we have left undone.
We ask to be forgiven.
By the power of your Spirit
turn us from evil to good,
help us to forgive others,
and keep us in your ways
of righteousness and love;
through Jesus Christ our Lord. Amen

Assurance of Pardon

Our sins are forgiven for his sake.
Thanks be to God.
Save us from the time of trial and deliver us from evil

Tuesday

> Christ be with me, Christ within me,
> Christ behind me, Christ before me,
> Christ beside me, Christ to win me,
> Christ to comfort and restore me.
> Christ beneath me, Christ above me,
> Christ in quiet, Christ in danger,
> Christ in hearts of all that love me,
> Christ in mouth of friend and stranger. Amen.

Wednesday

> Help us, God of truth and mercy,
> to act justly, to love tenderly,
> and to walk humbly with you,
> this and every day. Amen.

> *For the kingdom, the power and the glory are yours,*
> *now and for ever. Amen.*

HYMN

Tuesday—470 in *Rejoice and Sing*, "Christ who knows all his sheep"
Wednesday—410 in *Rejoice and Sing*, "Our Father God, thy name
we praise"

DOXOLOGY

THE GRACE

> The grace of our Lord Jesus Christ,
> and the love of God,
> and the fellowship of the Holy Spirit,
> be with us all evermore. Amen.

EVENING PRAYER ON TUESDAY

*Liturgy from W. E. Orchard, The Order of Divine Service, 1926,
Eighth Order for Evening Prayer.*[4]

SCRIPTURE SENTENCE

INVOCATION

CONFESSION:

> Almighty and most merciful Father;
>
> we have erred and strayed from thy ways like lost sheep.
>
> We have followed too much the devices and desires of our own hearts.
>
> We have offended against thy holy laws.
>
> We have left undone those things which we ought to have done;
>
> and we have done those things which we ought not to have done.
>
> But thou, O Lord, have mercy upon us.
>
> Spare thou them, O God, which confess their faults.
>
> Restore thou them that are penitent;
>
> according to thy promises declared unto mankind in Christ Jesus our Lord.
>
> And grant, O most merciful Father, for his sake;
>
> that we may hereafter live a godly, righteous, and sober life,
>
> to the glory of thy holy Name. Amen.

ABSOLUTION

THE LORD'S PRAYER

> Our Father, which art in heaven . . .
>
> O give thanks unto the Lord.
>
> Sing praises unto him; glory in his holy Name.

HYMN

> 206 in *Rejoice and Sing*, "With joy we meditate the grace"

4. London: OUP, 1926.

PSALM 15

O Lord, who may abide in your tent?
Who may dwell on your holy hill?
Those who walk blamelessly, and do what is right,
and speak the truth from their hearts;
who do not slander with their tongue,
and do no evil to their friends,
nor take up a reproach against their neighbors;
in whose eyes the wicked are despised,
but who honor those who fear the Lord;
who stand by their oath even to their hurt;
who do not lend money at interest,
and do not take a bribe against the innocent.
Those who do these things shall never be moved.
Glory be to the Father, and to the Son,
and to the Holy Spirit;
as it was in the beginning, is now,
and ever shall be, world without end. Amen.

LESSON

Hebrews 7:26–8.2; 9:11–14, 24–28

SCRIPTURE RESPONSE

The Beatitudes
After each verse . . .
Grant us this grace, we beseech thee, O Lord.

VERSICLES

Peace be with you.
And with all people.
Let us pray.
Glory to God in the highest;
On earth peace, good will towards men.
May the Almighty Lord order our days and our times in his
peace.
May the Lord grant us his peace and eternal life.
May the souls of the departed, through the mercy of God,

find a place of repose, refreshment and light.
Eternal rest give to them, O Lord.
Let light perpetual shine upon them.
And may they rest in peace.

INTERCESSIONS

Hear us, we beseech thee.

HYMN

27 in *Rejoice and Sing*, "Hail, gladdening Light"

BENEDICTION

EVENING PRAYER ON WEDNESDAY

*Liturgy from Presbyterian Church (USA),
Book of Common Worship, 1993*[5]

Jesus Christ is the light of the world,
the light no darkness can overcome.
Stay with us, Lord, for it is evening
and the day is almost over.
Let your light scatter the darkness
and illumine your church.

SCRIPTURE SENTENCE

EVENING HYMN

51 in *Rejoice and Sing*, "The duteous day now closes"

PSALM 141

I call upon you, O Lord; come quickly to me;
give ear to my voice when I call to you.
Let my prayer be counted as incense before you,
and the lifting up of my hands as an evening sacrifice.
Set a guard over my mouth, O Lord;
keep watch over the door of my lips.

5. Louisville and London: Westminster/John Knox, 1993, see "Evening Prayer," 505–23. Used with permission. Psalm 141 © New Revised Standard Version.

Do not turn my hear to any evil,
to busy myself with wicked deeds
in company with those who work iniquity;
do not let me eat of their delicacies.
Let the righteous strike me;
let the faithful correct me.
Never let the oil of the wicked anoint my head,
for my prayer is continually against their wicked deeds.
When they are given over to those who shall condemn them,
then shall they learn that my words were pleasant.
Like a rock that one breaks apart and shatters on the land,
so shall their bones be strewn at the mouth of Sheol.
But my eyes are turned towards you, O God my Lord;
in you I seek refuge; do not leave me defenseless.
Keep me from the trap that they have laid for me,
and from the snares of evildoers.
Let the wicked fall into their own nets
while I alone escape.
I call upon you, O Lord; come quickly to me;
give ear to my voice when I call to you.
Let my prayer be counted as incense before you,
and the lifting up of my hands as an evening sacrifice.

Scripture Reading

1 Corinthians 14:13–15, 26–33, 37–40
The Word of the Lord.
Thanks be to God.

Canticle

Nunc dimittis—742 in *Rejoice and Sing*, the third setting

Prayers of Thanksgiving and Intercession

To you, O Lord, I lift my soul.
O God, in you I trust.
Our Father, who art in heaven . . .

Hymn

501 in *Rejoice and* Sing, "I greet thee, who my sure Redeemer art"

Dismissal

> May the peace of God, which surpasses all understanding,
> guard our hearts and minds in Christ Jesus. **Amen.**
> Bless the Lord.
> **The Lord's name be praised.**

SERVICE OF THE WORD AND THE LORD'S SUPPER

Liturgy from Worship: from the United Reformed Church, 2003[6]

The Preparation

Greeting and Sentence

> Grace to you and peace from God our Father
> and the Lord Jesus Christ.
> **Grace to you and peace.**
> Our help is in the name of the Lord,
> **who made heaven and earth.**

Hymn

> 661 in *Rejoice and Sing*, "How shall I sing that majesty?"

Prayer of Approach

> 2a in *Rejoice and Sing*

The Great Commandment

> Hear, O Israel:
> **The Lord our God, the Lord is one.**
> Love the Lord your God
> with all your heart, with all your soul,
> with all your mind, and with all your strength.
> **This is the first and the great commandment.**
> The second is like it: Love your neighbor as yourself.
> **There is no commandment greater than these.**

Prayer of Confession

> All have sinned and fall short of the glory of God.
> Jesus says: I have come to call not the righteous but sinners.

---

6. London: © The United Reformed Church, UK, 2003.

Let us together confess our sins in penitence and faith and seek
God's forgiveness.

Almighty God, we confess before you
our own sin, the sin of the Church
and the sin of the world, in which we share.
We have not loved you with our whole being;
we have not loved our neighbor as ourselves.
In your mercy, forgive us when we turn from you;
release us from the burden of our past,
and remake us in your image and likeness
through Jesus Christ our Lord. Amen.

Assurance of Forgiveness and Call to Discipleship

The Lord says, See, I am making all things new.
If anyone is in Christ, there is a new creation.
In Christ God was reconciling the world to himself.
Through him your sins are forgiven.
Amen. Thanks be to God.
The Lord also says:
If any want to become my followers, let them deny themselves
and take up their cross and follow me.

Kyrie eleison
5b in *Rejoice and Sing*

The Ministry of the Word

Before Scripture is read the minister says

Lord, break the bread of your word among us
and nourish us with your truth.
Hebrew Scriptures—Isaiah 6:1–8
Hear the word of the Lord.
Thanks be to God.
New Testament—Revelation 4:1–11
Hear the word of the Lord.
Thanks be to God.

Psalm 24—681 in *Rejoice and Sing*, "Ye gates, lift up your heads on high"

Gospel—John 4:7–26

Hear the word of the Lord.
Thanks be to God.

Reflection

The Response

Prayers of Intercession

Offertory Hymn

454 in *Rejoice and Sing*, "Let all mortal flesh keep silence"

THE LORD'S SUPPER

Invitation

The Peace

The Offering of Bread and Wine

Response twice . . . **Blessed be God for ever.**
Then . . .
Blessed are you, Lord, God of all creation.
Through your goodness we have ourselves to offer,
fruit of the womb, and formed by your love.
May we become your servants in the world.
Blessed be God for ever.

The Thanksgiving

Lift up your hearts.
We lift them to the Lord.
Let us give thanks to the Lord our God.
It is right to give our thanks and praise.
The Eucharistic Prayer continues . . .
Therefore with all your people in heaven and on earth
we sing the triumphant hymn of your glory:
Holy, holy, holy Lord,
God of power and might,
heaven and earth are full of your glory.
Hosanna in the highest.
Blessed is he who comes in the name of the Lord.
Hosanna in the highest.
The Eucharistic Prayer continues . . .

Let us proclaim the mystery of faith:
Dying, you destroyed our death.
Rising, you restored our life.
Lord Jesus, come in glory.
The Eucharistic Prayer concludes

The Lord's Prayer

Agnus Dei

14 in *Rejoice and Sing*

The Communion

Holy things for a holy people.
Only one is holy, the Lord Jesus Christ.
We are made holy in him.

Prayer after Communion

God of a love stronger than death,
you have given us new birth into a living hope
through the gift of your Son.
God with us,
like a mother you have fed us with yourself
and strengthened us for journeying ahead.
God of truth and power,
you take our weakness and our sin
and refashion us by grace.
Gracious God,
may the love which bids us welcome at this table
gather all your children into one,
in your eternal presence,
whole and free at last. Amen.

Hymn

709 in *Rejoice and Sing*, "New songs of celebration render"

Dismissal

Go out into the world with the food of your pilgrimage in
peace and gladness.
Thanks be to God for his gift beyond words.

Blessing

Bibliography

Ainslie, James L. *The Doctrines of Ministerial Order in the Reformed Churches of the Sixteenth and Seventeenth Centuries*. Edinburgh: T & T Clark, 1940.

Anglican-Reformed International Commission. *God's Reign and Our Unity*. London: SPCK, 1984.

Aquinas, Thomas. *Summa Theologica, Part I*. Translated by the Fathers of the English Dominican Province. 2nd ed. London: Burns, Oates & Washbourne, 1920.

Aulén, Gustav. *Eucharist and Sacrifice*. Edinburgh: Oliver & Boyd, 1958.

Baptist Union of Great Britain. *Gathering for Worship: Patterns and Prayer for the Community of Disciples*. Norwich: Canterbury Press, 2005.

———. *Orders and Prayers for Church Worship: A Manual for Ministers*. London: Carey Kingsgate Trust, 1960.

———. *Patterns and Prayers for Christian Worship: A Guidebook for Worship Leaders*. Oxford: OUP, 1980

Barkley, John M. *The Worship of the Reformed Church*. London: Lutterworth, 1966.

Barrow, Henry. *The Writings of Henry Barrow, 1587–1590*, edited by Leland H. Carson. London: Allen & Unwin, 1962.

Barth, Karl. *Homiletics*. Louisville: Westminster/John Knox, 1991.

———. *The Knowledge of God and the Service of God According to the teaching of the Reformation*. London: Hodder & Stoughton, 1938.

———. *The Proclamation of the Gospel*. London: SCM, 1964.

———. "Revelation." In *Revelation*, edited by J. Baillie and H. Martin, 41–81. London: Faber & Faber, 1937.

Barth, Karl, et al. *Revolutionary Theology in the Making: The Barth-Thurneysen Correspondence, 1914–25*. Louisville: Westminster/John Knox, 1964.

Best, Thomas F., and Heller, Dagmar. *Eucharistic Worship in Ecumenical Contexts: The Lima Liturgy and Beyond*. Geneva: WCC, 1998.

Binfield, Clyde. *The Contexting of a Chapel Architect: James Cubbitt, 1836–1912*. London: The Chapels Society, 2001.

———. *So Down to Prayers: Studies in English Nonconformity, 1780–1920*. London: J M Dent, 1977.

———. "Profile: Geoffrey Nuttall: the Formation of an Independent Historian." *Epworth Review*, xxv, 1 (1998) 79–106.

Boyd, Kenneth M. *Scottish Church Attitudes to Sex, Marriage and the Family, 1850–1914*. Edinburgh: John Donald, 1980.

Brilioth, Yngve. *Eucharistic Faith and Practice: Evangelical and Catholic*. London: SPCK, 1965.

Calvin, John. *Brève Instruction chrétienne*. 1537. Translated by Stuart Olyott as *Truth for all Time—A Brief Outline of the Christian Faith*. Edinburgh: Banner of Truth, 2008.

———. *Institutes of the Christian Religion.* Edited by John T. McNeill, Translated by Ford Lewis Battles, 2 volumes, The Library of Christian Classics, Volumes XX and XXI. Philadelphia: Westminster, 1960.

———. *Institutes of the Christian Religion.* Translated by H. Beveridge. Grand Rapids: Eerdmans, 1989.

———. *Theological Treatises.* Translated by J. K. S. Reid, The Library of Christian Classics, Volume XXII. London, SCM Press, 1954.

Causse, Jean-Daniel. "Reprendre et Commencer." In *Etudes Théologiques et Religieuses,* (2005/4) 543–54.

Christian Reformed Church. *Psalter Hymnal.* 1957. Reprint. Grand Rapids: CRC Publications, 1976.

———. *Psalter Hymnal.* Grand Rapids: CRC Publications, 1987.

Church of England. *Book of Common Prayer.* 1662. Reprint. Cambridge: CUP, 2004.

———. *Eucharistic Presidency: A Theological Statement by the House of Bishops of the General Synod.* London: Church House Publishing, 1997.

Churches Together in Britain and Ireland. "The Report of the British Council of Churches Study Commission on Trinitarian Doctrine Today." In *The Forgotten Trinity, British Council of Churches Commission on Trinitarian Doctrine Today.* 1989. Reprint. London: CTBI, 2011.

Clark, Francis. *Eucharistic Sacrifice and the Reformation.* London: Darton, Longman & Todd, 1960.

Clark, Neville. "The Fullness of the Church of God." In *The Pattern of the Church: A Baptist View,* edited by Alec Gilmore, 79–113. London: Lutterworth Press, 1963.

Concise Oxford Dictionary. 11th ed. Oxford: OUP, 2008.

Congregational Union of England and Wales. *Year Book.* London: CU, 1931.

Cornick, David. "Twentieth-Century Historians of English Protestant Nonconformity." In *Protestant Nonconformity in the Twentieth Century,* edited by A. P. F. Sell and A. Cross, 63–78. Carlisle: Paternoster, 2003.

———. *Under God's Good Hand: A History of the Traditions which have Come Together in the United Reformed Church in the United Kingdom.* London: URC, 1998.

Dale, Robert W. *A Manual of Congregational Principles.* 9th ed. London: Hodder & Stoughton, 1902.

Daly, Robert J. *The Origins of the Christian Doctrine of Sacrifice.* London: Darton, Longman & Todd, 1978.

Davies, Horton. *Bread of Life and Cup of Joy: Newer Ecumenical Perspectives on the Eucharist.* Leominster: Gracewing, 1993.

———. *Worship and Theology in England: from Andrewes to Baxter and Fox, 1603–1690.* Princeton: Princeton University Press, 1975.

———. *Worship and Theology in England: from Newman to Martineau, 1850–1900.* London: OUP, 1962.

Dix, Gregory. *The Shape of the Liturgy.* London: A & C Black, 1978.

Douglas, Barbara. "Prayers made with song: the Genevan Psalter, 1562–1994." In *Pledges of Jubilee: Essays on the Arts and Culture, in Honor of Calvin G. Seerveld,* edited by L. Zuidervaart and H. Luttikhuizen, 285–307. Grand Rapids: Eerdmans, 1995.

Duffy, Eamon. *The Stripping of the Altars: Traditional Religion in England, 1400–1580.* London: Yale, 1992.

Durber, Susan. "An Inclusive Communion Order for a Denominational Worship Book." In *Presiding like a Woman,* edited by N. Slee and S. Burns, 38–47. London: SPCK, 2010.

Eire, Carlos M. N. *War Against the Idols.* Cambridge: CUP, 1986.

Forrester, Duncan B, and Murray, Douglas. *Studies in the History of Worship in Scotland.* 2nd ed. Edinburgh: T & T Clark, 1996.

Forrester, Duncan B. et al. *Encounter with God: An Introduction to Christian Worship and Practice.* 2nd ed. Edinburgh: T & T Clark, 1999.

Forsyth, Peter T. *The Cruciality of the Cross.* 2nd ed. London: Independent, 1948.

———. *Faith, Freedom, and the Future.* London: Independent, 1955.

———. *Lectures on the Church and the Sacraments.* London: Longmans, 1917.

———. *Positive Preaching and the Modern Mind.* 2nd ed. London: Hodder & Stoughton, 1909.

Garside, Charles. "The Origins of Calvin's Theology of Music, 1536–1543." *Transactions of the American Philosophical Society,* 69.4 (1979) 1–36.

Gassmann, Günther. *Documentary History of Faith and Order: 1963–1993.* Faith and Order Paper 159. Geneva: WCC, 1993.

Green, H. Benedict. *Lay Presidency at the Eucharist?* Affirming Catholicism. London: Darton, Longman & Todd, 1994.

Greene-McCreight, Kathryn. "What's the Story? The Doctrine of God in Common Order and the Book of Common Worship." In *To Glorify God: Essays on Modern Reformed Liturgy,* edited by Bryan Spinks and Iain Torrance, 99–114. Edinburgh: T & T Clark, 1999.

Gunton, Colin E. *The Theology of Reconciliation.* London: T & T Clark, 2003.

Hall, David D. *The Works of Jonathan Edwards: xii, Ecclesiastical Writings.* New Haven: Yale University Press, 1994.

Hanson, Richard P. C. *Eucharistic Offering in the Early Church.* Bramcote: Grove Books, 1979.

Harris, Ruth. *Lourdes: Body and Spirit in the Secular Age.* London: Allen Lane, 1999.

Hart, Darryl G. *Recovering Mother Kirk: The Case for Liturgy in the Reformed Tradition.* Grand Rapids: Baker Academic, 2003.

Hastings, Adrian. "God." In *The Oxford Companion to Christian Thought,* edited by A. Hastings et al, 269–74. Oxford: OUP, 2000.

Herron, Andrew. *The Law and Practice of the Kirk: A Practical Guide and Commentary.* Glasgow: Chapter House, 1995.

Holmes, Andrew R. *The Shaping of Ulster Presbyterian Belief and Practice, 1770–1840.* Oxford: OUP, 2006.

Hunter, John. *Devotional Services for Public Worship.* 5th ed. Glasgow: James Maclehose & Sons, 1892.

James, Edwin O. *Sacrifice and Sacrament.* London: Thames & Hudson, 1962.

Jasper, Ronald C. D., and Cuming, Geofrey J. *Prayers of the Eucharist: Early and Reformed.* 2nd ed. New York: OUP, 1980.

———. *Prayers of the Eucharist: Early and Reformed.* 3rd ed. Minnesota: Liturgical Press, 1990.

Jones, Cheslyn. et al. *The Study of the Liturgy.* London: SPCK, 1992.

Kaye, Elaine. "Henry Allon." In *Dictionary of National Biography.* Oxford: OUP, 2004. Online: http://www.oxforddnb.com/view/article/411.

———. *Mansfield College, Oxford, its Origin, History, and Significance.* Oxford: OUP, 1999.

Kaye, Elaine, and Mackenzie, Ross. *W. E. Orchard—A Study in Christian Exploration.* Oxford: Education Services, 1990.

Keck, Leander. E. *The Bible in the Pulpit—the Renewal of Biblical Preaching.* Nashville: Abingdon, 1979.

Lewis, Clive S. *Letters to Malcolm: Chiefly on Prayer*. New York: Brace Jovanovich, 1964.

Locke, John. *An Essay Concerning Human Understanding*, Book III, §34. Oxford: OUP, 2008.

Long, Thomas G. "The Distance We Have Travelled: Changing Trends in Preaching." In *A Reader on Preaching. Making Connections*, edited by David Day et al., 11–16. Aldershot: Ashgate, 2005.

Lovibond, Malcolm. "A Matter of Indifferency: A Commentary on the Cheshire Classis Meetings of 1691." *Journal of the United Reformed Church History Society* viii, 4 (June 2009) 197–209.

Macarthur, Arthur. *Setting Up Signs: Memories of an Ecumenical Pilgrim*. London: URC, 1997.

MacLaren, A. Allan. *Religion and Social Class: The Disruption Years in Aberdeen*. London: Routledge & Kegan Paul, 1974.

Marvin, Ernest. *Shaping Up: Re-forming Reformed Worship*. London: URC, 2005.

Maxwell, William D. *Concerning Worship*. Oxford: OUP, 1949.

———. "Worship in the Reformed Church." *The Journal of the Presbyterian Historical Society of England*, viii, 4 (1947) 123–37.

Mazza, Enrico. *The Origins of the Eucharistic Prayer*. Minnesota: Liturgical Press, 1995.

———. *The Celebration of the Eucharist: The Origins of the Rite and the Development of Its Interpretation*. Minnesota: Liturgical Press, 1999.

McFague, Sallie. *Speaking in Parables*. Philadelphia: Fortress, 1975.

McLaughlin, William M., and Pinnock, Jill. In *Mary for Earth and Heaven: Essays on Mary and Ecumenism*. Leominster: Gracewing, 2002.

Meyerhoff, Steven. "Pioneer of Reformed Worship—Celebrating the 500th Anniversary of Martin Bucer." Online: http://www.reformedworship.org/magazine/article. cfm?_id=579.

Molnar, Paul D. *Divine Freedom and the Doctrine of the Immanent Trinity*. London: T & T Clark, 2002.

Morgan, John, and Strudwick, Vincent. *The Way of Salvation*. Faculty Monograph Series. Oxford: OUP, 1999.

Moltmann, Jürgen. "The Motherly Father and the Power of his Mercy." In *History and the Triune God*, 19–25. London: SCM Press, 1991.

Moule, Charles F. D. *The Sacrifice of Christ*. London: Hodder & Stoughton, 1956.

Mudge, Lewis S. *Rethinking the Beloved Community*. Geneva: WCC, 2001.

Nichols, Aidan. *The Holy Eucharist*. Dublin: Veritas, 1991.

———. "The Holy Oblation: On the Primacy of Eucharistic Sacrifice." *The Downside Review* 122 (2004) 259–72.

Nuttall, Geoffrey F. *The Holy Spirit in Puritan Faith and Experience*. Oxford: Basil Blackwell, 1946.

Old, Hughes O. *Worship that is Reformed according to Scripture*. Atlanta: John Knox, 1984.

Parry, Kenneth L., and Routley, Eric. *Companion to Congregational Praise*, London: Independent Press, 1953.

Presbyterian Church (USA). *Book of Order*. Louisville: Westminster/John Knox, 2007.

Presbyterian Church of England, *The Book of Order*. 7th ed. London: PCE, 1964.

———. *Directory for the Public Worship of God*. London: PCE, 1894.

Ramsey, Michael. *The Gospel and the Catholic Church*. London: Longmans, Green & Co, 1936.

Reid, J. K. S. *Calvin: Theological Treatises*. London: SCM, 1954.

Rice, Howard L, and Huffstutler, James C. *Reformed Worship*. Louisville: Genevan, 2001.

Ricoeur, Paul. "Biblical Hermeneutics." *Semeia* 4 (1975) 29–148.

———. "Creativity in Language: Word, Polysemy, Metaphor." *Philosophy Today* 17.2 (1973) 97–111.

———. *Du texte à l'action. Essais d'herméneutique II*. Paris: Editions du Seuil, 1986.

———. *Freud and Philosophy: An Essay on Interpretation*. Translated by D. Savage and T. Lectures. New Haven: Yale University Press, 1970.

———. "The Hermeneutical Function of Distanciation." *Philosophy Today* 17 (1973) 129–41.

———. "The Hermeneutics of Symbols and philosophical reflection 1." In *The Conflict of Interpretations: Essays on Hermeneutics*, edited by D. Ihde, 284–311. Translated by D. Savage. Evanston: Northwestern University, 1974.

———. "Metaphor and the Central Problem of Hermeneutics." In *Hermeneutics and the Human Sciences: Essays on Language, Action, and Interpretation*, edited by John B. Thompson, 165–81. Cambridge: CUP, 1981.

———. *Oneself as Other*. Translated by K. Blamey. Chicago: University of Chicago Press, 1992.

———. "Preface to Bultmann." In *The Conflict of Interpretations: Essays in Hermeneutics*, edited by D. Ihde, 381–402. Translated by P. McCormick. Evanston: Northwestern University, 1974.

———. "Le Royaume dans les paraboles de Jésus." *Etudes Théologiques et Religieuses*, supplément hors-série 2005/4 (1976/1) 31–37.

———. *The Rule of Metaphor: Multi-Disciplinary Studies of the Creation of Meaning in Language*. Translated by R. Czerny et al. London: Routledge, 2003.

Roberts, A., and Donaldson J. *The Ante-Nicene Fathers Translations of the Writings of the Fathers down to A.D. 325. Volume I: The Apostolic Fathers, Justin Martyr, Irenaeus*. Grand Rapids: Eerdmans, 1969.

———. *The Ante-Nicene Fathers Translations of the Writings of the Fathers down to A.D. 325. Volume V: Hippolytus, Cyprian, Caius, Novatian, Appendix*. Grand Rapids: Eerdmans, 1971.

Rupp, Gordon. *Patterns of Reformation*. London: Epworth, 1969.

Schaff, Philip. *The Nicene and Post-Nicene Fathers of the Christian Church. Series I. Volume XIV: St Chrysostom: Homilies of the Gospel of St John and the Epistle to the Hebrews*. Grand Rapids: Eerdmans, 1969.

Schmidt, Leigh E. *Holy Fairs: Scotland and the Making of American Revivalism*. 2nd ed. Grand Rapids: Eerdmans, 2001.

The Scottish Psalter, London: OUP, 1929.

Sell, Alan P. F. *Saints: Visible, Orderly and Catholic: The Congregational Idea of the Church*. Geneva: World Alliance of Reformed Churches, 1986.

Sheikh, Bilquis. *I Dared to Call Him Father*. Eastbourne: Kingway, 2001.

Shuster, Marguerite. "The Triune God." In *Exploring and Proclaiming the Apostles' Creed*, edited by Roger E. Van Harn, 1–12. Grand Rapids: Eerdmans, 2004.

Slack, Kenneth. *The United Reformed Church*. Exeter: Religious & Moral Education Press, 1978.

Soskice, Janet M. *Metaphor and Religious Language*. Oxford: OUP, 1985.

———. "Trinity and Feminism." In *The Cambridge Companion to Feminist Theology*, 135–150. Cambridge: CUP, 2002.

Spinks, Bryan. *From the Lord and "the Best of the Reformed Churches": a Study of the Eucharist in the English Puritan and Separatist Traditions.* Rome: CLV Edizioni Liturgiche, 1984.

Sternhold, Thomas, and Hopkins, John. *The Whole book of Psalms, collected into English Metre.* London: John Day, 1562.

Stiver, Dan R. *Theology after Ricoeur: New Directions in Hermeneutical Theology.* Louisville: Westminster/John Knox, 2001.

Sykes, Norman. *Old Priest and New Presbyter: Episcopacy and Presbyterianism since the Reformation with especial relation to the Churches of England and Scotland.* Cambridge: CUP, 1956.

Tate, Nahum, and Brady, Nicholas. *A New Version of the Psalms of David,* London: E James, 1754.

Temple, William. *Nature, Man and God.* London: Macmillan, 1934.

Thomasset, Alain. "L'imagination dans la pensée de Paul Ricoeur: Fonction poétique du langage et transformation du sujet." *Etudes Théologiques et Religieuses* (2005/4) 525–41.

Thompson, David M. "The Irish Background to Thomas Campbell's 'Declaration and Address'". *Journal of the United Reformed Church History Society* 5 (1985) 215–25.

———. *Stating the Gospel: Formulations and Declarations of Faith from the Heritage of the United Reformed Church.* Edinburgh: T & T Clark, 1990.

Thurian, Max. *Ecumenical Perspectives on Baptism, Eucharist and Ministry.* Faith and Order Paper No 116, Geneva: WCC, 1985.

Townsend, C.M. *The Mind of John Gibb.* London: Nisbet, 1923.

Troeltsch, Ernest. *Social Teaching of the Christian Churches.* English translation by Olive Wyon, London: Allen & Unwin, 1931

Tucker, Tony. *Reformed Ministry: Traditions of Ministry and Ordination in the United Reformed Church.* London: URC, 2002.

United Reformed Church. *The Manual,* 6th ed. London: URC, 2000.

———. *Record of the General Assembly.* London: URC, 1973–2007.

———. *Rejoice and Sing,* Oxford: OUP, 1991.

———. *Reports to the General Assembly.* London: URC, 1973–95.

———. *Worship: from The United Reformed Church.* London: URC, 2003 and 2004.

Warr, Charles L. *The Presbyterian Tradition.* London: Alexander Maclehose & Co, 1933.

Watson, Francis. "Hermeneutics and the Doctrine of Scripture: why they need each other." *International Journal of Systematic Theology,* 12/2 (2010) 118–43.

Watts, Isaac. *Hymns and Spiritual Songs.* New ed. London: J Barfield, 1811.

Watts, Michael R. *The Dissenters: from the Reformation to the French Revolution.* Oxford: OUP, 1978.

White, Erin. "Between suspicion and hope: Paul Ricoeur's vital hermeneutics." *Journal of Literature and Theology,* 5/3 (1991) 311–24.

White, James F. *Introduction to Christian Worship.* Nashville: Abingdon, 1980.

White, Susan. *Whatever Happened to the Father? The Jesus Heresy in Modern Worship.* London: Methodist Sacramental Fellowship, 2002.

Williams, Jane. "The Fatherhood of God." In *The Forgotten Trinity, British Council of Churches Commission on Trinitarian Doctrine Today,* 166–175. 1991. Reprint. London: CTBI, 2011.

Williams, Rowan. *Eucharistic Sacrifice: The Roots of a Metaphor.* Bramcote: Grove Books, 1982.

Young, Frances M. *Sacrifice and the Death of Christ.* London: SPCK, 1975.

Index